CW01594016

access English 1

TEACHER'S RESOURCE FILE

Jill Baker · Clare Constant · David Kitchen

Heinemann
Inspiring generations

Heinemann Educational Publishers,
Halley Court, Jordan Hill, Oxford OX2 8EJ.
Part of Harcourt Education Ltd.

Heinemann is the registered trademark of Harcourt Education Ltd.

First published 2003

07 06 05
10 9 8 7 6 5 4 3 2

British Library Cataloguing in Publication Data is available
from the British Library on request

ISBN 0 435 22595 2

Designed and produced by Bridge Creative Services Limited, Bicester, Oxon
Printed in the UK by Athenaeum Press Ltd
Original illustrations © Reed Educational & Professional Publishing 2003
Illustrations by Kathryn Baker, Kathy Baxendale, Karen Donnelly, Alice Englander, Tony Forbes, Phil Healey, Pantelis Palios, Nick Schon, Lisa Smith, Martin Ursell, Sarah Warburton, Geoff Ward, Jennifer Ward

Acknowledgements
Every effort has been made to trace copyright holders of material reproduced in this book. Any omissions will be rectified in subsequent printings if notice is given to the publishers.

Extracts from: *Truth Or Dare* by Celia Rees, published by Macmillan. Reprinted with permission of Macmillan; from *Rude Health* by Linda Aronson, published by Macmillan, Copyright © Linda Aronson, 1999. Reproduced by permission of Macmillan Children's Books, London, UK, Linda Aronson, and Macmillan Australia; from 'There's No Such Thing' by Paul Jennings from *Unbelievable,* published by Penguin Books, Australia, and reprinted with permission of the publishers; from *Face* by Benjamin Zephaniah, published by Bloomsbury. Copyright © Benjamin Zephaniah, 1999. Reprinted with permission of Bloomsbury; from *Minders* by Diana Hendry, published by Walker Books. Copyright © 1998 Diana Hendry. Reproduced by permission of Walker Books Limited, London.

The publishers would like to thank the following for permission to reproduce the following photographs on page 136: Tony Stone/Getty Images (Teenage skateboarder); Empics (Boy playing football).

Tel: 01865 888058 www.heinemann.co.uk

Contents

Introduction

Welcome to ***Access English***, a comprehensive resource for low attainers in English at Key Stage 3.

Access English is designed to cover National Curriculum requirements and the objectives of the Framework for Teaching English while prioritising those objectives that are most important for these students. The programme reflects all that is best about the teaching sequence and approaches of the Progress and Foundation Units.

Book 1 targets students progressing from National Curriculum level 2 and securing level 3 while covering the Framework's Year 7 objectives.

Book 2 enables students to consolidate National Curriculum level 3 and progress towards level 4 while covering the Framework's Year 8 objectives.

Book 3 enables students to move beyond level 3 to achieve and consolidate National Curriculum level 4 while covering the Framework's Year 9 objectives.

Access English provides:

- learning and teaching strategies that move students towards independence
- development of students' thinking skills
- explicit teaching and articulation of invisible thinking and decision-making processes used when reading, writing, speaking or listening
- integration of reading and writing, speaking and listening
- progression across each book and across the course
- a highly motivating ICT component to improve both English and ICT skills
- quality texts chosen for their high interest and accessible language level
- stimulating activities to help students enjoy learning.

The material is designed to ensure that students know what they have learned and are able to see themselves making real progress, helping to build their self-esteem.

We hope you enjoy using ***Access English*** and seeing your students realise more of their full potential.

Jill Baker *Clare Constant* *David Kitchen*

Teaching and learning with *Access English*

Access English components

Access English level	Year	National Curriculum level	Components		
1	7	2–3	Student book	Teacher's Resource File	Student CD-ROM
2	8	(2) 3 (4)	Student book	Teacher's Resource File	Student CD-ROM
3	9	3–4	Student book	Teacher's Resource File	Student CD-ROM

Student Book

Part A: Investigating Literature

Part B: Investigating Non-fiction

- Parts A and B consist of eighteen skills-based ***units*** which focus on the comprehension and composition of non-fiction, literary and oral texts. Each unit comprises a series of linked ***sections*** that target relevant objectives.
- Each ***section*** enables students to learn and consolidate skills by benefiting from the underpinning teaching sequence: remember, model, try, apply, secure.

However, ***Access English*** is not prescriptive. It is designed so that teachers can use it flexibly, depending on their class's circumstances, while still gaining full benefits from the resources.

Suggested five-part teaching sequence

1 Making links

- At the beginning of each section, students work as a class with the teacher.
- Students may be asked to recall relevant prior knowledge, e.g. *what they already know about writing paragraphs*. This allows the teacher to:
  – focus students' attention on the skill being addressed
  – get a picture of individual student's current understanding
  – give students confidence.
- Students may do preparatory tasks, e.g. *securing the meaning of vocabulary that will be used later* or *identifying key features of a text*.

2 Whole class

- Part 2 focuses on the main objective(s) being addressed in the section. An annotated model text is provided in the student book (and where needed, also supplied, without annotations, in the Teacher's Resource File (TRF) so that teachers can copy it to an OHT).
- Reading the text and discussing the annotations enables teachers to explain and model the key skill for students. Tasks and/or questions allow teachers to demonstrate and then share the act of composition or comprehension with students.
- Active reading is encouraged wherever possible by positioning the questions and tasks *before* the annotated text.

3 Supported practice

- In part 3, students work in pairs or small groups to try out the skill they are developing in a carefully scaffolded context. This is an opportunity for teachers and learning support staff to focus on individual pairs/groups or groups of pairs/groups.
- At the end of this part of the teaching sequence teachers may wish to draw the class together again to consolidate skills, and check on achievement and understanding before students work independently.

4 Independent work

- The tasks in part 4 provide an opportunity for students to work independently to consolidate the skills they have been practising.

5 Securing the skills

- In part 5, students come together as a class to secure the skills that have been learnt. Activities may include:
  - sharing work and discussing how it was done using the skills that have been practised
  - sharing composition or comprehension of a text with the teacher, who makes the process explicit to consolidate learning.

Part C: Investigating Words

This section covers the key spelling objectives from the Word level strand for Year 7. Many students working below the expected National Curriculum level need to learn a range of independent spelling strategies and useful ways to remember. They also need enough information to make their 'best guess' when they do not know how to spell a word. This section includes useful strategies for the students to learn. Subsequent pages refer back to these strategies as appropriate. Students should be prompted to apply these strategies in all their independent writing across the curriculum.

Each page begins with a target statement for the pupils, followed by information and/or spelling rules and conventions. There are then a series of activities which allow pupils to explore the spelling objective. There is a strong emphasis on equipping the pupils with spelling strategies which they can apply, as well as learning useful spelling rules and conventions.

The spelling pages are designed to be used in a range of ways.

- **Whole class:** when a whole class is working at a similar level, each page could be used as a series of starter activities during a week of English lessons.
- **Differentiated activities in a mixed attainment class:** in this situation, the information would form part of the whole class teaching. Each page then offers a choice of activities for pupils working below the expected National Curriculum level. Several of the activities should be used over a series of lessons to consolidate learning.
- **Revision:** the activities could be used to revise earlier learning. In most cases, there is a need for some direct teacher input and modelling of how to apply the strategies.

Features used in the Student Book

Symbols

WS There is a worksheet for this activity

IW There are starter activities related to this word or phrase (part C, Student Book)

Remember boxes remind students of important ideas already learnt:

> **Remember**
> If you don't know some of the words opposite, use a dictionary to find out what they mean.

Key term boxes define the meaning of a key term used in the unit:

> **Key term**
>
> **predict** – to guess what will happen next based on what you know

Teacher's Resource File

Unit guides

The unit guides are easy to use and provide all the information needed to teach the unit.

To facilitate short-term planning, the ***unit*** begins by setting out:

- the objectives covered within the unit
- the resources provided to support teaching.

To enable teachers and students to get the most out of each ***section*** of the unit, the guide identifies:

- the objectives targeted by that section
- the worksheets and material that can be copied to OHTs which support individual activities
- how the five-part teaching sequence works.

In addition, the unit guide offers:

- teaching tips – the teacher may select from these, or adapt them to suit the individual class
- answers where appropriate
- suggestions for consolidation and extension.

Worksheets

These are designed to give students additional support while they practise the skills that have been explained and demonstrated to them; they may also be used to support differentiation within a class.

Some worksheets are provided where an alternative way of teaching the same skill is suggested in the TRF, or where an activity in the Student Book lends itself to marking or cutting up a text.

Sheets that can be copied to OHTs (OHT sheets)

These are intended to support teachers in part 2 of the suggested teaching sequence (**Whole class**). At this point the teacher works with the whole class using the text to focus on the main objectives being taught. A copy of the text used in the Student Book, without annotations, is usually supplied as a sheet in the TRF that can be copied to an OHT. This is so that the teacher can annotate the text on the OHT while explaining and modelling the key skill to students. The OHT may also be used to support the shared writing or reading tasks in this part of the teaching sequence. In the Student Book the text is usually annotated so that students can refer back to it as they practise the skills themselves.

Homework sheets

These are complete in themselves so that students don't need to take the Student Book home. They provide an opportunity for students to reinforce/consolidate specific skills in their own time. The activities are short, interesting and designed to be achievable by students working independently.

Self-assessment sheets

These provide the opportunity for students to reflect on what they have achieved at the end of each unit, to diagnose areas that need further development and to set themselves realistic, achievable targets that are agreed with their teacher. The self-assessment sheets are likely to be most useful if preceded by discussion of the work covered in the unit and the students' response to it.

Strategy bank

This is a photocopiable bank of resources which can be used in a number of different ways. Each card in the strategy bank gives students strategies to try in a particular situation – such as when planning a text or when the student does not understand a word.

The strategy bank can be used in a number of ways:

- students can be given a card to jog their memories as they tackle a particular task
- the cards in the bank can be loosely bound in a folder so that students can use it like a book. Then they can decide which card they need to use in a particular situation
- the bank can be photocopied onto OHTs for whole class teaching
- the cards can be used as the basis for lesson starters, recapping strategies already taught
- the cards can be used to teach strategies.

Framework matching chart

The chart is intended to facilitate long-term and medium-term planning. It is designed so teachers can easily see:

- in which unit a specific objective is first taught or revisited
- how objectives are clustered within units.

Student CD-ROM

The Student CD-ROM includes animations, sound, video and texts, and offers:

- carefully structured activities that target skills developed in the Student Book
- opportunities for individual, paired and whole class work
- lively animations to encourage and motivate students
- combined text, sound and images to support learners working independently
- structured support for writing
- reinforcement of learning using instant on-screen feedback.

1 Shaping stories

Student Book pages 4–15

Support for this unit
- Worksheets 1.1–1.5
- OHT sheets 1.1–1.2
- Homework sheet 1.1
- Self-assessment sheet
- CD-ROM activities

Teaching and learning focus
- Telling a story
- Understanding how stories are structured
- Structuring and writing a story

Objectives covered

Sentence level
- 3 Boundary punctuation
- 4 Tense management
- 8 Starting paragraphs

Text level – Reading
- 7 Identify main ideas
- 15 Endings

Text level – Writing
- 1 Drafting process (planning)
- 2 Planning formats
- 5 Story structure

Speaking and Listening
- 2 Recount

1.1 Telling stories

Objectives S3, S&L2

1 Making links

1, 2 Recounting stories they have told or heard shows students that they are already experienced storytellers. This activity could be extended by discussing:
- who tells stories on TV – comedians, chat show guests, etc.
- what features make someone an effective storyteller.

2 Whole class

Model text: Transcript of an oral recount

OHT 1.1 supports this activity

1 Help students to see how a recount usually answers five questions: When? Where? Who? What? Why?

2 Check understanding of the model by asking: i) **When** did it happen? **Who** is the story about? etc. or ii) How does the speaker give the information?

3 Supported practice

Worksheet 1.1 supports this task

1 Students work in pairs to recount orally a story told in a picture. Tell them *not to write down* their ideas as the emphasis is on telling, not reading, an anecdote.

2 Students can practise telling their story to each other before trying it out on another pair. This could lead to feedback on:
– whether all the points are covered
– use of voice – loud, clear, etc. – as well as expression
– use of language – how to put in amusing/interesting details.

4

Independent work

Worksheet 1.1 could be used again to support this task

1, 2 Students tell a story of their own to a partner, using the five questions to help them plan. Teachers may wish to model this task by telling a story, then asking students to answer the questions: When? Who? Where? What? Why?

3 After telling the story to a partner, stories can be shared in larger groups or told by more confident students to the rest of the class who give feedback.

5

Securing the skills

- The class is asked to recapitulate the five things to say when telling a story.

1.2

How writers shape stories

Objectives R7, R15

N.B. There is no independent work in this section.

1

Making links

- Students list what they expect writers to do when writing a story. At this point it is useful if they can discuss the 'beginning, middle, ending' structure encountered in Key Stages 1 and 2. This task provides an opportunity to establish what students already know about story writing. Students can be asked to indicate which things on the list they have tried to do in their own story writing. The list may also broaden their understanding of what they can aim for.

2

Whole class

Model text: *Cinderella* set out as a chart

Worksheet 1.2 supports this activity

- Use the chart with its example of *Cinderella* to introduce students to the idea of stories having five stages. (The simplified explanations of each stage in the chart correspond to: opening, development, complication, crisis and resolution.)
- This is an opportunity to examine the similarity in structure of other well known stories, e.g. *fairy stories*: *Red Riding Hood, Goldilocks and the Three Bears*; *legends, e.g. Jonah and the Whale, Noah's Ark*; *film stories, e.g. James Bond plots.*

1 Point out that not all stories rely on withholding information to maintain the reader's interest. However, it is a favourite device in mysteries, thrillers, and in many urban myths (*Boo!*, *The Back Seat* and the plot of *The Choking Dog* are examples of urban myths).

2 Examine the structure of the short story *Boo!* with the students.

Stage 1 (*Who?*) A girl is (*Where?*) in an old house (*When?*) on the day her father goes to London.

Stage 2 (*What happens?*) Her father goes to London. (*Why is this a problem?*) She doesn't want to sleep in the house on her own.

Stage 3 (*Someone tries to sort out the problem. Who?*) The girl tries to make sure she is safe. She makes sure no one is in the house. She locks up carefully.

Stage 4 (*Things get worse. How?*) Bedtime comes. She has to turn off the light and try to go to sleep.

Stage 5 (*Things sort out – happily or unhappily. How?*) The person hiding in the house shows s/he is there. Unfortunately the girl has locked them both in her room.

3 The writer withheld the information that someone was hidden in the girl's bedroom right until the end. This produced a surprise ending for readers to enjoy.

3 **Supported practice**

Worksheet 1.2 supports this activity

1, 2 Read the story with the students, stopping at the end of each stage to let students complete sentences to explain what stage they have just read, e.g.:

1 *This is the opening. It tells you the story is about Rachel, at two o'clock one night after a party; she is in town.*

2 *What happens is Rachel drives home. Rachel is frightened by a truck driver who keeps flashing his lights at her. This causes a problem because she is frightened.*

3 *Rachel tries to sort out the problem by driving home as fast as she can and by sounding her horn when she gets home to wake her dad up.*

4 *Things get even worse because the driver of the truck gets out and says there is a man with an axe in the car with Rachel.*

5 *This is the conclusion. Things are sorted out happily when Rachel's father gets her out of the car and the truck driver grabs the man with the axe who was hiding in her car. The ending works well because Rachel is safe.*

4 **Securing the skills**

- Students are asked to recall and explain to a partner the five stages of a story.

1.3 Planning a story

Objectives Wr1, Wr2, Wr5, S&L2

1 **Making links**

1 Students discuss differences between writing and telling a story. Points to include: a) more complex structure is possible in written stories; b) spoken stories generally give less detail, written stories can have more description, character development, detail about setting, more careful word choice, etc.; c) written stories are generally for a wider unknown audience, spoken stories for a smaller, known audience (except on TV etc.).

2 Students recap the five stages of written stories from section 1.2.

2 **Whole class**

Model text: Story plan with surprise ending: dog had stolen the hidden present

Worksheet 1.2 supports this activity

- Model using the five stages to plan a story.

1 Students are asked to suggest a different ending and piece of hidden information, e.g. *Conclusion*: Gran (introduced earlier in the story) comes downstairs playing with the Game Boy Advanced; *Hidden information*: Gran had already found it under the sofa.

3 **Supported practice**

Worksheet 1.3 supports this activity

- Students sequence five pictures to plan a five-stage story. They may produce a variety of sequences. Check that their stories follow the structure before they do the independent work.

4 **Independent work**

Worksheet 1.2 supports this activity

- Students write the plan of their story in a chart format.

5 **Securing the skills**

- Students are asked to recap what to do when planning a story. They should refer to the five stages and explain how these help them plan a story. They could also read each other's plans in pairs or share them with the rest of the class.

1.4 Writing a story

Objectives S3, S4

N.B. This section can still be used by students who missed section 1.3.

Homework sheet 1.1 supports these activities

1 **Making links**

1 Help the students to share what they know about the past tense. When brainstorming examples, try to elicit different past tenses from the class: *went, was going, had gone,* etc.

2 Students share what they already know about writing in sentences. If they can suggest strategies for making sure a sentence is a sentence, the whole class work can arise out of their suggestions/experience.

2 **Whole class**

Model text: Flow chart for writing in sentences

- Demonstrate how to think up, check and write sentences. If this is a new strategy, model it several times before students share in the writing process.

1 Reinforce this by asking students to explain the strategy.

2 Ask students to write three more sentences for the opening of the scene. Initially the teacher may act as scribe while students suggest alternatives for the first sentence. However, they should try to write their last sentence independently before it is re-written on the OHT/whiteboard for the whole class to examine.

3 **Supported practice**

Worksheet 1.4 supports this activity

- In pairs, students write in sentences to complete a paragraph of the story, following steps 1–4.

4 **Independent work**

Worksheet 1.4 supports this activity

- Students write five more sentences telling the next stage in the story based on artwork repeated from the previous section.

5 **Securing the skills**

- Pairs of students read and mark each other's sentences, reinforcing their understanding of sentences and boundary punctuation. The teacher could also write a version of the five sentences with the class so that the whole class can discuss and correct the process.

1.5 Writing in paragraphs

Objective S8

N.B. This section can still be used by students who missed section 1.4.

1 **Making links**

- Students share what they already know about writing in paragraphs.

2 **Whole class**

Model text: Annotated story showing paragraph use

OHT 1.2 supports this activity

- Explain why new paragraphs are needed and demonstrate how a new paragraph is begun. Students work out why the writer began a new paragraph each time: *The writer wrote about: a different place, then a different person, then a different person who speaks.* Explain how speech is written: when someone different speaks, their words go on a new line.
- Emphasise that paragraphs help readers follow the sequence of ideas in a text. They are visual clues, showing that the next piece of text is about a different idea or topic.

3 **Supported practice**

Worksheet 1.5 supports this activity

1, 2 In pairs, students decide and explain where new paragraphs are needed. At least six are definitely needed, but others may be felt necessary by students.

4 **Independent work**

- Students write the final paragraphs of the story based on artworks repeated from 1.3.

5 **Securing the skills**

- Students recall what they know about writing in paragraphs. They refer to their completed texts and explain to the class why they chose to begin a new paragraph.

Worksheet
1.1

Student Book
Unit 1 • page 5

Listening to a story

Read through this checklist first. Make sure you understand what you are listening for. Then listen to someone telling their story.

1 Write their name at the top of a column.

2 Put a tick or a cross in each box to show how well they tell their story.

Name of speaker:				
Did you find out:				
When it happened?				
Who it is about?				
Where it happened?				
What happened?				
Why the person felt like that?				
Is the speaker speaking:				
loudly enough?				
clearly?				
slowly?				
Did you **enjoy** the story?				

Worksheet
1.2

Student Book
Unit 1 • pages 6–11

The five stages of a story

Story stages	Story ______
1 Opening The scene is set: *Who? When? Where?*	
2 Development Something happens that causes a problem: *What?* *Why is this a problem?*	
3 Someone tries to sort out the problem: *Who?* *How?*	
4 But things get even worse: *How?*	
5 Conclusion Things get sorted out – happily or unhappily: *How are they sorted out?*	

Worksheet

1.3 Planning a story

Student Book
Unit 1 • page 11

Work in pairs. Cut out the five pictures. Then decide what order they need to go in to tell a story.

Worksheet

1.4 Writing a story

Student Book
Unit 1 • page 13

3 **Work in pairs to write the *four* missing sentences below. Take it in turns to say a sentence out loud. Check with your partner that it makes sense. Then write the sentence down.**

Karen wanted to find somewhere to live. It had ____________________

____

She had looked in the newspaper for somewhere to rent. ____________________

____.

She could not afford much. ____________________

____.

She had phoned up the landlord. ____________________

____.

4 **Now write *five* sentences on your own. Tell the next part of the story.**

____

____

____

____

____

____

____

____

Worksheet

1.5

Beginning new paragraphs

udent Book
1 • page 15

3

Work in pairs.

1 Read the text below.

2 Where should this writer have started a new paragraph? Find *at least six* places. Mark each place with the symbol /. The first one has been done for you.

New paragraph needed because writing about a different place.

Karen did not like the look of Mark Kreep very much. He had a shaved head and a strange smile. If she took the flat she hoped she would not have to see him very often. / Mark showed her round the flat. It had everything Karen wanted but it was very dirty. When they were outside again she said, 'It's okay but it needs cleaning.' Mark looked at her and said, 'I would get it cleaned before you move in.' Karen thought carefully. The rent was okay. She could make the flat look nice. 'I'll take it,' she said. Later she told her dad about the flat. He was very worried. 'That's a very rough part of town. Will you be safe?' he asked. That got Karen thinking.

3 Explain why a new paragraph is needed each time.

New paragraph (line 4) needed to show writing about a different place.

New paragraph

OHT 1.1

Spoken stories

Student Book
Unit 1 • page 4

Night fright

Last night I was asleep and I woke up suddenly ... and I was sure there was someone trying to get into my bedroom ... I could see this black thing coming through the curtain and I was really scared ... I couldn't do anything ... I couldn't even yell ... then the black thing jumped on my bed – it was the cat.

OHT

1.2 Writing in paragraphs

Student Book
Unit 1 • page 14

Flat hunt

It was very early in the morning. Karen had to be at the flat by ten o'clock and she did not know the way. She saw the sign for Leeds Town Centre and came off the motorway.

Half an hour later Karen spotted 47 Wilting Gardens. It was in a rough part of town. That was why the flat was so cheap to rent.

Mark Kreep was waiting outside when she got there. He smiled and said hello.

'Hello,' said Karen.

Homework
1.1

Student Book
Unit 1 • pages 12–13

Writing sentences

Name

What you have to do

Write *five* sentences about a time you felt scared.

Make sure **each** sentence:

- makes sense
- begins with a capital letter
- ends with a full stop.

1 Plan your ideas first.

2 Write your *five* sentences.

I was ____

Shaping stories – how did I do?

Name

Think about the work you have done on telling, reading and writing stories. Tick the boxes to show what you are able to do.

In this unit:	I found this easy	I could do this with some help	I found this very difficult. I need to get better at this
1 I told a story.			
2 I read a story and found the five stages.			
3 I planned a five-stage story.			
4 I wrote in sentences.			
5 I wrote in paragraphs.			

I was best at ____________________

I need to improve ____________________

I will do this by ____________________

Signed ____________________

2 Active reading

Student Book pages 16–21

Support for this unit
- Worksheet 2.1
- OHT sheet 2.1
- Homework sheet 2.1
- Self-assessment sheet
- CD-ROM activities

Teaching and learning focus
- Visualising a scene
- Predicting what will happen
- Inference and deduction of meaning

Objectives covered

Text level – Reading
- 6 Active reading
- 8 Infer and deduce
- 17 Independent reading

Text level – Writing
- 2 Planning formats
- 3 Exploratory writing

Speaking and Listening
- 1 Clarify through talk

2.1 Finding evidence in the text

Objectives R6, R8

1 **Making links**

- Students recall how their favourite story starts. Try to make links with various types of stories, also with films. Find out if any students have worked with a professional storyteller.

2 **Whole class**

OHT 2.1 supports this activity

Model text: First paragraph of *Truth or Dare* by Celia Rees

1, 2 Students read the text and look at the illustration. Allow them to find only one fact (thing they definitely know), one correct item from the picture and one incorrect item. They can then find the rest in the next section.

- Mark the fact on OHT 2.1. Facts include: *Josh in mother's car; sunny weather; July; on busy motorway; holiday traffic; caravans and trailers on road; Josh not going on holiday*. Allow 'Josh is being kidnapped' as a fact if students assert it, but return to the issue in activity 5.

3 **Supported practice**

1, 2 Encourage students to work briskly in pairs to find other things they definitely know, and other mistakes in the picture.

4 **Independent work**

- Work individually to list the facts. Concentrate on clarity, brevity and helpful layout. Discourage copying of text as it is the student's words that matter.

5 **Securing the skills**

OHT 2.1 supports this activity

- In sharing and checking the facts, start by dealing with the things that are not open to debate – it is July and not December. Highlight key words that indicate what is happening.
- Address briefly what might be the boy's opinion rather than a fact. Look at the last sentence and the idea that he is being 'kidnapped'. Explain that the next session will look at what might be happening.

2.2 Predict what might happen

Objectives R6, R8, Wr3

1 **Making links**

- Recap what you found out in section 2.1 (see checklist under activity 2).

2 **Whole class**

Model text: First paragraph of *Truth or Dare* by Celia Rees

- Explain that prediction is a key aspect of reading fiction. Readers want to know what is going on. We read on to find out what happens, to see if we were right about characters and what is happening to them.
- Deal with annotations one at a time. Quickly collect as many ideas as possible, quality irrelevant. Then sift them. Try to reach agreement or at least a strong majority view on each of the four annotations.

3 **Supported practice**

- Read over the new piece of text with the group. Ask the pairs to look for clues here just as you did together with the earlier piece of text. Circulate to check that pairs remain on task.
- The 'clues' from which students might predict include: *mum's face, frowning and tense; mum's fingers, drumming steering wheel; car full of gear.*

4 **Independent work**

- Students have three sentence openings to complete. Stress the need to create as much detail in the predictions as possible, e.g.:

  Josh is going to ... his uncle's house – but why? what is it like? what is his uncle like? why is his mum nervous?

5 **Securing the skills**

- Get as many students as possible to share their predictions. A few details from many are better than many details from a few. Reinforce the term **prediction**.
- Most students will want to know how close they got in their predictions. Josh is actually being taken to his Nan's house. Nan has had a stroke and Mum is going up to help. She is tense about Nan's health and also about going back to a place of which she has painful memories.

2.3 Making sense of a text

Objectives R6, R8, R17, Wr2, S&L1

1 **Making links**

- This section links together the deduction of section 2.1 with the inference of section 2.2 and makes explicit use of those terms.
- Predicting what will happen in a story, film or TV programme, especially a soap, will be an everyday experience for most students, even if they have never articulated it before. Concentrate on how definite different students felt about their predictions and why.

2 **Whole class**

Model text: Extract from *Bad Girls* by Jacqueline Wilson

▸ ***Worksheet 2.1 supports this activity by providing a copy of the chart***

1 Read story opening once.

- Introduce chart and the words *deduction* and *inference* from the chart.
- Link them with their subheadings which explain the terms.
- Ask about where to put the statements in the chart.
- Read the passage again and confirm or change where the statements go.

3 **Supported practice**

▸ ***Worksheet 2.1 supports this activity***

▸ ***Homework sheet 2.1 reinforces this activity***

1, 2 Get pairs to return to the text as they form their judgements.

- Some students will say that they are definite about everything. Get them to consider alternative explanations: for example, the girls could have been simply waiting for the bus and have spotted Mandy.
- Make sure that every student is filling in their own chart.

4 **Independent work**

Worksheet 2.1 supports this activity by providing a copy of the chart

- Students complete the charts on their own. Those who finish the charts first should
5 check and review their judgements. Ask them to be ready to give reasons later.

Securing the skills

1 Get a range of opinions about where things fit in the chart. Whatever the opinion, draw out the reasoning behind it.

2 Answers suggested are:

Deduction: *This happens outside school; Mandy wears sandals; it happens after school has finished for the day; Kim is the worst bully.*

Inference: *The teachers don't know about the bullying; the other girls have been waiting to get Mandy; the bullying has been going on for some time.*

3 Give the students a few minutes to learn the meaning of the important terms *deduction* and *inference*.

Worksheet
2.1

Making sense of a text

Student Book
Unit 2 • page 20

Use this chart to complete activities 2, 3 and 4 on pages 20–21.

Deduction *(What I can work out definitely)*	**Inference** *(What I can guess about what is going on)*

Evidence in the text

Joshua on the move

The last place Joshua Parker wanted to be on a sunny day in late July was sitting in a car, stuck in heavy traffic, heading north on the M1. Cars towing trailers and caravans clogged the lane in front, almost bringing it to a standstill. Holiday traffic. But Josh was not going on holiday. He was being driven away from his friends, his summer, kidnapped by his own mother.

Taken from *Truth or Dare* by Celia Rees

Can you be sure?

Name

What you have to do

1 **Read the text below. Decide which statements are *definitely* true.**

2 **Write your own explanation.**

The head teacher drove up to school in a white Rolls Royce. The students were amazed. He stepped out of the car and smiled. He was wearing a bright white suit and a pink tie.

'He's won the lottery,' said one student.

'He's gone mad,' said another.

'He was always mad,' said a third.

The head of lower school, Mrs Hope, came across. She whispered in his ear. They both laughed.

Then the head produced a massive cigar and put it in his mouth. The students could not believe it. He was always going on about the dangers of smoking.

1 **Underline the statements that are *definitely* true.**

A The head teacher was wearing a white suit.

B The head teacher had won the lottery.

C The head teacher had gone mad.

D The head teacher was wearing a pink tie.

E The head teacher listened to Mrs Hope.

F The head teacher was enjoying himself.

G The head teacher liked cigars.

H The head teacher came to school in a Rolls Royce.

I The head teacher owned a Rolls Royce.

J The head teacher often told students that smoking was dangerous.

2 **Write your own explanation. Say what *you* think has happened to the head teacher.**

Active reading – how did I do?

Name	

Think about the work you have done on active reading.

Tick the boxes to show what you are able to do.

In this unit:	I found this easy	I could do this with some help	I found this very difficult. I need to get better at this
1 I pictured what is happening in a story.			
2 I predicted what might happen next in a story.			
3 I gave reasons for my predictions.			
4 I told the difference between what I definitely knew and what I thought might be happening.			

I was best at ____________________

I need to improve ____________________

I will do this by ____________________

Signed ____________________

3 Understanding fiction

Student Book pages 22–29

Support for this unit
- Worksheet 3.1
- OHT sheet 3.1
- Homework sheet 3.1
- Self-assessment sheet
- CD-ROM activities

Teaching and learning focus
- Responding to fiction
- Relating responses to reader's own experience
- Characterisation

Objectives covered

Word level
- 14 Word meaning in context
- 16 Unfamiliar words

Sentence level

Text level – Reading
- 1 Locate information
- 2 Extract information
- 6 Active reading
- 9 Distinguish writer's views
- 17 Independent reading

Text level – Writing
- 2 Planning formats
- 3 Exploratory writing

Speaking and Listening
- 1 Clarify through talk

3.1 How the narrator feels

Objectives W14, W16, R6, R9, R17

1 Making links

1 Stress that everyone meets words they do not understand. Emphasise that there is no need to panic.

2 Adults work out meanings mostly from context. A dictionary clarifies/makes certain.

2 Whole class

Model text: Extract from *Blabbermouth* by Morris Gleitzman

1 Ask for stories about something that went wrong for a friend. Move the story on from what happened to how the storyteller felt about what had happened: *guilty, embarrassed, sorry, amused, superior, etc.*

2 The model-text incident takes place in a stationery cupboard in an Australian school.

3 The narrator: *is tense; feels stupid; has lost control; feels in big trouble.*
- Key phrases you can highlight about the narrator's situation: *so dumb; messed up ... so totally and completely; a knot in my guts the size of Tasmania.*

3 Supported practice

1,2 Choice of the four best words is up to the pairs of students. Some are arguably stronger for this situation than others:
- *foolish* is reasonable but *childish* captures particularly well the sense that she has done something silly or immature
- the narrator may well be *shy* but there is better evidence for saying she is *scared.*

4 Independent work
- Students can expand on how they think the narrator might be feeling. Stress the need for full sentences here.
- ***Extension***: students can come up with their own words to describe the situation and use those in sentences.

5 **Securing the skills**

- Look for how the sentence relates to the adjective chosen. A sentence like this may be expected: *I felt **silly** because of what I had done.* A sentence like this makes a stronger connection to the adjective used: *I felt **shocked** because I didn't think I could get into so much trouble so quickly.*
- Brainstorm possible reasons for the narrator's predicament. This both reinforces the work on how characters feel and prepares the way for the next section.

3.2 How characters feel

Objectives Wr3, S&L1

1 **Making links**

OHT 3.1 supports this activity

Model text: Extract from *Blabbermouth* by Morris Gleitzman

1. Discuss not being able to speak, like Rowena. Students are usually much more matter-of-fact about disability than adults. Almost everyone has some disability: eyesight, bad back, poor hand–eye coordination. Rowena's difficulty is larger and so requires greater effort to overcome.
2. Read the extract preamble and the extract with the students. Encourage the students to answer the questions in the annotations. If they find this difficult, suggest: What would you feel if you were Rowena/a student in the class/the teacher? Scribe their ideas on OHT 3.1.

2 **Whole class**

- Talk briefly about the nature of *empathy*. Relating this to the better known word *sympathy* can help. However, concentrate not on the word, but on how the characters may be feeling. A range of views is acceptable here.
- Each student should record their own ideas and some ideas that come out of the subsequent discussion.

3 **Supported practice**

- Play the teacher yourself in this first run through, or choose an able/enthusiastic actor from the group. You can try more than one student in the role of the student who wants to help. The role of Rowena is ideal for students who are uneasy about their verbal abilities.

4 **Independent work**

- Allow the students to allocate the three parts initially. Reserve the right to switch the parts around swiftly if it is not working or in order to see how people react to different roles. Make sure that each student gets a chance to try playing all three roles. Encourage them to evaluate the performances and to bring one or two good ideas to the class discussion in **5**.

5 **Securing the skills**

- Allow time to listen to at least two dialogues. Compare and contrast, taking the best from both performances. Use the spider diagram to recap/reinforce the ideas arising from the role plays.

3.3 Responding to characters

Objectives R1, R2, R6, R17, Wr2, S&L1

Homework sheet 3.1 supports this section

1 Making links

Model text: Extract from *Dakota of the White Flats* by Philip Ridley

Information for brainstorming activity: Dakota:

- is ten years old
- does Saturday work in a market
- is hard-working
- lives with mum
- is a person who sorts things out
- has a mind of her own.

2 Whole class

Worksheet 3.1 supports this activity

1 Students do not have to agree with either of the artist's impressions. These questions explore how our imaginations embellish the bare facts when reading to create an overall response as readers.

2 Students should record the factual detail that has been collected. Other aspects of the profile are for the class to decide.

3 Supported practice

As a parallel process to **3.3.1**, students talk about Henry Twig. We know that he is:

- 28 years old
- tall
- thin
- unemployed
- lazy
- uses a toothpick
- afraid of silverfish.

4 Independent work

Worksheet 3.2 supports this activity

- Students now use the information they have extracted from the text to write a profile of Henry Twig. They will need to supplement this with ideas of their own, giving them the opportunity to start creating a character. Make sure each student is producing their own profile and not simply copying their partner's ideas. Challenge factual matters, but encourage diversity in imaginative response.

5 Securing the skills

1 Students share their ideas; make sure they hear several versions. Henry Twig could be illustrated either alongside profile or on class whiteboard.

2 Ask students to describe how they worked out their characters.

Worksheet

3.1

Student Book
Unit 3 • page 29

Responding to characters

Profile: Dakota Pink

Age	
Size	
Height	
Face	
Hair	
Clothes	
Shoes	
Work	
Behaviour	
Habits	
Talk	
Other details	

Worksheet
3.2

Student Book
Unit 3 • page 29

Responding to characters

Profile: Henry Twig

Age	
Size	
Height	
Face	
Hair	
Clothes	
Shoes	
Work	
Behaviour	
Habits	
Talk	
Other details	

OHT

3.1 How characters feel

Student Book
Unit 3 • page 25

Rowena

Teacher

Students

Homework
3.1

Student Book
Unit 3 • page 29

Creating a character

Name

What you have to do

1 Write a profile of a person who could become a character in a story. You can:

- make up your person
- base your person on someone you know
- base your person on different parts of several people.

Your character **must** have a made up name: ____________________

Answer these ten questions to help you create your character.

1 How old is your person? ____________________

2 How tall are they? ____________________

3 What sorts of clothes do they wear? ____________________

____

4 What does their face look like? ____________________

____

5 What do they do each day? ____________________

____

6 What is their favourite food? ____________________

7 What do they like to do in their free time? ____________________

8 How do they speak? ____________________

____

9 Who are their friends? ____________________

____

10 What is unusual or special about them? ____________________

____

____

____

Understanding fiction – how did I do?

Name	

Think about the work you have done about characters in stories.

Tick the boxes to show what you can do.

In this unit:	I found this easy	I could do this with some help	I found this very difficult. I need to get better at this
1 I described a character.			
2 I found the right words to describe how a character would feel.			
3 I wrote my own profile of a character.			
4 I created a character of my own.			

I was best at ____________________

I need to improve ____________________

I will do this by ____________________

Signed ____________________

4 Describing characters

Student Book pages 30–41

Support for this unit
- Worksheets 4.1–4.3
- OHT sheet 4.1
- Homework sheet 4.1
- Self-assessment sheet
- CD-ROM activities

Teaching and learning focus
- Understanding how characters are conveyed
- Using descriptions, actions and dialogue to show what a character is like
- Drafting skills

Objectives covered

Word level
- 14 Word meaning in context
- 17 Word classes

Sentence level
- 7 Speech punctuation
- 18 Sentences in older texts

Text level – Reading
- 12 Character, setting and mood
- 16 Author attitudes

Text level – Writing
- 1 Drafting process (planning)
- 6 Characterisation
- 9 Link writing and reading

4.1 Understanding characters

Objective R12

1 **Making links**

- Students brainstorm clues writers give readers about what a character is like, e.g. *description, actions, speech*. Use the opportunity to recap on inference and deduction from unit 3.

2 **Whole class**

Model text: Description of Mr Berkhoff from *Rude Health* by Linda Aronson

OHT 4.1 supports this activity

1 Explain and demonstrate how to find and interpret clues about a character in a text. Students complete two inferences: *People feel afraid of him; His words show that he is angry and in charge*.
2 Together, students and teacher read and analyse the clues in another piece of text. Emphasise the difference between what Berkhoff actually does and what Ian thinks he *could* do – which shows us how Ian feels about him.

3 **Supported practice**

Worksheet 4.1 supports this activity

- In pairs, students read a text by Paul Jennings describing Sister Gribble. They say whether they agree with a reader's thoughts about each paragraph, and give reasons. Model answers: *1 Agree; 2 Disagree – Sister Gribble is not pretty, or generous (she has mean eyes [that] look like slits on money boxes ...); Agree – she is smart and tidy; 3 Agree; 4 Disagree – the grandson dislikes her calling Grandad 'the old man'. It shows a lack of care for their feelings.*

4 **Independent work**

1 Students list the five clues they need to search for to find out what a character is like.
2 Then they recall the two questions that help readers work out what a writer is saying about a character: *What do I definitely know? What can I work out or guess?*

5 **Securing the skills**

1,2 Students work with the teacher using the same techniques to tackle a short extract from a pre-twentieth century text.

4.2 Describing a character's looks

Objectives W17, Wr1, Wr6, Wr9

1

Making links

1, 2 Students play a miming game to explore how a person's appearance, e.g. expression, gives clues about what they are feeling.

2

Whole class

Model text: Extract describing the head teacher from *Rude Health* by Linda Aronson

1 Students recap the skills they learnt in the previous section by reading the description of a character's appearance and working out what the character is like.

2 The teacher demonstrates how to use ideas in a flowchart to work out a description of a character (a happy person).

3

Supported practice

Worksheet 4.2 supports this activity

1, 2 In pairs, students use the flowchart to plan ideas for describing a teacher. Students must jot down the ideas independently. They may find it easier if it is suggested that they choose an unpleasant character to describe.

4

Independent work

- Students write a paragraph describing the character they planned. The teacher may decide to model turning notes into full sentences before students attempt this work. A writing frame is provided to support this task.

5

Securing the skills

1, 2 In pairs, students read each other's descriptions. The writer should explain why the details were chosen. This is also an opportunity for the class to examine the use of details in a successful text or to suggest improvements to a less successful text.

4.3 Writing about what a character does

Objectives W14, W17, Wr1, Wr6, Wr9

1

Making links

- Students play a game like charades using different feelings and actions. This is to develop students' understanding of how emotions are expressed by actions in preparation for their reading.

2

Whole class

Model text: two extracts from *Remote Man* by Elizabeth Honey

- Use the text and questions to explore how a writer chooses words describing actions carefully to reveal characters' feelings.

1 *a) Ned is feeling angry (defiant): 'hacked off ... cheese ...'; carries on watching television, deliberately not doing homework. b) Ned doesn't care about healthy eating.*

2 *a) Mum is angry (furious? frustrated?): she flings a frying pan at the TV screen. b) She is the one who does the cooking; she acts 'suddenly' – her action is unexpected; she is unpredictable.*

3 *'Flung' is a better word than 'threw' because it shows that she threw the frying pan really hard and angrily.*

- Discuss the fact that both characters feel angry but show it in different ways.

3

Supported practice

Worksheet 4.3 supports this activity

1 Students are reminded that it is verb phrases and adverbs that convey what a character is feeling.

2 In pairs, students choose the best words to describe a shy, nervous character.

4 **Independent work**

- Students write a paragraph describing the actions of a character – either the English teacher they described earlier, or Ned from the extract on page 38.

5 **Securing the skills**

- Help the class to pick out the actions that show how the character is feeling in the students' descriptions.

4.4 Writing speech

Objectives W14, S7, Wr6

Homework sheet 4.1 supports this section

1 **Making links**

1 Students share what they already know about punctuating speech. Key ideas: *speech marks around the words spoken; new line for each change of speaker.*

2, 3 Students brainstorm and demonstrate different ways of speaking. Generate a list of different words for 'said' to use in activity **4**.

2 **Whole class**

Model text: Extract from *Dangerous Reality* by Malorie Blackman

1, 2 Students read a conversation and apply what they have learnt. *1) Mike 'smiled' - he's friendly; 'sighed' - he's had enough of Mum's forgetfulness; 'Mike gave ... a wry look verging on disapproval' – he doesn't like Dominic's sense of humour. 2) Dominic is winding Mike up. He's someone who enjoys teasing people.*

3, 4 Use the short extract provided to demonstrate how to set out speech.

3 **Supported practice**

1, 2 In pairs, students act out the rest of the conversation between Mike and Dominic, including another example of how Dominic might wind Mike up. Encourage them to use different ways of speaking, in preparation for activity **4**.

4 **Independent work**

- Students write up the conversation they improvised, punctuating carefully and indicating how the words are spoken. As they are encouraged to use alternative words to 'said', the list they made in activity **1** should be available.

5 **Securing the skills**

- Students work in pairs to correct each other's speech punctuation. They could also work in pairs to read out finished conversations, making their speech sound like the words describing it suggest.

Worksheet

4.1 Understanding characters

Student Book
Unit 4 • page 32

Sister Gribble

On Monday I went to the nursing home where they kept Grandad. I had to wait for ages in this little room which had hard chairs and smelt of stuff you clean toilets with. The nurse in charge wore a badge which said, SISTER GRIBBLE.

1 I'm looking at her name.
The nurse is a sister so she is important. When you say her name it sounds quite fierce. She might be scary.

1 We agree/disagree because ________________________________

____

She had mean eyes. They looked like the slits on money boxes which take things in but never give anything back. She had her hair done up in a tight bun and her shoes were so clean you could see the reflection of her knobbly knees in them.

2 I'm looking at what she looks like.
Sister Gribble is pretty. She looks like a kind and generous person. She is smart and tidy.

2 We agree/disagree because ________________________________

____

'Follow me, lad,' said the nurse after ages and ages. She led me down a corridor and into a small room. 'Before you go in,' she said, 'I want you to know one thing. Whenever the old man talks about things that are not really there, you must say, "There's no such thing." You are not to pretend you believe him.'

3 I'm looking at how she speaks, what she says, and how she behaves.
Sister Gribble is bossy. She doesn't want to walk with him and chat.

3 We agree/disagree because ________________________________

____

I didn't know what she was talking about, but I did know one thing – she shouldn't have called Grandad 'the old man'. He had a name just like everyone else.

Taken from *There's No Such Thing* by Paul Jennings

4 I'm looking at how she makes others feel.
The grandson thinks Sister Gribble is doing a good job. She really seems to care about about how he and his Grandad feel.

4 We agree/disagree because ________________________________

____

Worksheet

4.2

Student Book
Unit 4 • page 35

Describing a character's looks

Step 1 Decide what kind of person he or she is:

angry happy sad shy enthusiastic
calm tired scared worried proud

Step 2 What animal is this kind of person most like?

Step 3 What does a person like this look like?

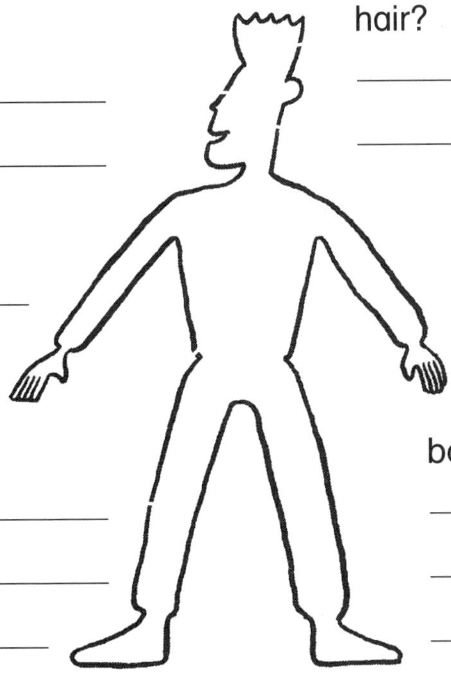

eyes?

____

____

hair?

____

____

mouth?

____

____

nose?

____

____

clothes?

____

____

____

body?

____

____

____

Step 4 Make up a good name for this sort of person.

e.g. *cheerful Milly Giggle* *proud Cecil Highborn*

____

Writing about what a character does

1 Work in pairs. Read the remember box.

Remember

You can show what a person is like by carefully choosing:

- action words (**verb phrases**):
  giggled *was afraid* *moaned* *roared* *went crazy*
- words which tell you how the action was done (**adverbs**):
  suddenly *slowly*

2 Fill in the blanks in the text below. Use words and phrases that show that Chong is shy and nervous. Choose words from the box below or use your own.

The loud music told Chong this was where the party was. He ____________ on the door and ____________ . At once the door burst open. 'Hi! You got here!' shouted Polly. Chong ____________ into the dark hallway. 'Hello,' he ____________ . Then he ____________ and stopped. Chong ____________ ____.

thumped	crept in	tapped	strode in	shuffled
waited	shouted	mumbled	went red	quietly
grinned	wished he hadn't come		felt excited	nervously

Understanding characters

Student Book
◆ pages 30–31

A

Mr Berkhoff

Ian is in Mr Berkhoff's maths lesson.

Mr Berkhoff gives a bloodcurdling roar. He chucks his bit of chalk at the back wall, charges from the blackboard to the front desk and bellows, 'That is enough!'

Dead silence. The bit of chalk is rolling across the floor somewhere. I'm terrified to breathe because I'm sitting in the front row with Berkhoff's enormous gut jammed up against my desk twenty centimetres from my eyes. I don't dare look upwards. He'll be frowning so hard his eyebrows will have merged into one thick black wavy line. He'll also be glaring around to see who chucked the pen top.

B

Mr Berkhoff is huge. He's tall and fat with a permanent scowl. He's sarcastic and he picks on people. He looks as if he could rip up phone directories with his bare hands. He looks as if he could rip up kids with his bare hands.

Taken from *Rude Health* by Linda Aronson

Homework

4.1

Punctuating speech

Student Book
Unit 4 • page 41

Name

What you have to do

1 **Read the text below.**

2 **Use opening quotes " or closing quotes " to show where the spoken words begin or end.**

3 **Put // every time the writer should begin a new line.**

So what brings you to our neck of the woods? Mike smiled. Mum forgot her key card. I know. Mike sighed. I had to issue her with a temporary one for the day. She'd forget her teeth if she didn't keep them in a glass by her bed, I told Mike. She sees them as soon as she wakes up each morning and yet sometimes I have to remind her that she's about to leave the house with only her gums on show! Mike stared at me. Your mum has false teeth?! I burst out laughing. You won't tell her I told you that, will you?

Describing characters – how did I do?

Name	

Think about the work you have done on understanding how writers describe characters and on describing your own characters.

Tick the boxes to show what you are able to do.

In this unit:	I found this easy	I could do this with some help	I found this very difficult. I need to get better at this
1 I found clues that showed what a character was like.			
2 I worked out what the clues I found meant.			
3 I noticed how an older text was punctuated.			
4 I decided whether a writer liked the character he described.			
5 I described how a character looked.			
6 I described how a character acted.			
7 I described how a character spoke.			
8 I punctuated the speech I wrote.			

I was best at ______________________________

I need to improve ______________________________

I will do this by ______________________________

Signed ______________________________

____

5 Staging scripts

Student Book pages 42–53

Support for this unit
- Worksheets 5.1–5.2
- OHT sheet 5.1
- Homework sheet 5.1
- Self-assessment sheet
- CD-ROM activities

Teaching and learning focus
- Developing drama techniques
- Responding to drama script
- Exploring characters in role
- Collaborative work/discussion

Objectives covered

Word level
- 6 Apostrophes

Sentence level
- 3 Boundary punctuation (exclamation marks)

Text level – Reading
- 18 Response to a play

Text level – Writing
- 6 Characterisation

Speaking and Listening
- 12 Exploratory talk
- 15 Explore in role
- 16 Collaborate on scripts
- 18 Exploratory drama
- 19 Evaluate drama presentations

5.1 Responding to scripts

Objectives R18, S&L12, S&L15, S&L16, S&L18, S&L19

1 **Making links**

- Examples of conflict can come from any source. Some may talk about sibling or playground rivalry. Do not push examples further than the students feel comfortable with. Link also with the dramas with which they are familiar – TV soaps, police series, hospital dramas.

2 **Whole class**

Model text: Extract of play about family conflict, from *End of the Road* by Kara May

- Read the script with the students. Possible responses to the questions:
  1. Why does Grandad keep on reading? *He doesn't want his reading interrupted; he doesn't like Sandy; he's been ignored all day so he's now ignoring Sandy.*
  2. How is he treating Sandy? *Making it clear he's not pleased; it's his/her parents he wants, not Sandy; he's giving Sandy a sense of not being important.*
  3. How does he look? *He's sour, bitter-looking; he looks miserable.*
  4. Is he pleased or sarcastic? *Sarcastic.*
  5. Is Sandy responding to his bad mood or ignoring it? *Ignoring it; trying to be cheerful.*

3 **Supported practice**

- Monitor the paired role playing. Choose good examples to show to the whole of the class. Ask questions about emphasis: *How difficult should Grandad be? How cheery should Sandy be?*

4 **Independent work**

- Students relate back to discussion in previous section, although this part of the script may change students' views. Possible responses to the annotations:

  1 Surprised? Annoyed? *probably just surprised.* 2 Sulking? Angry? *mainly a sulk at this stage; could be played as sheer amazement.* 3 Confused? Frustrated? *more frustration than confusion; perhaps feels that Grandad is confused.* 4 Appealing to him or angry? *an appeal to fairness with a hint of building towards anger.*

5 **Securing the skills**

- Ask every student to write down two or three words about the performance they are watching before discussing it. Everyone then has got at least one brief opinion to give. Look for: *believable characterisation; a sense of the building conflict.*

5.2 Developing the characters

Objectives S&L15, S&L16, S&L18, S&L19

1 Making links

- Discuss the two characters as a class. Points to make: Sandy is: *cheerful, practical, willing to stand up to Grandad, strong sense of what's fair, has a very busy job.* Grandad is: *looking for an argument, thinks his needs come before Sandy's, not reasonable.*

2 Whole class

Model text: Play extract based on above play

- Play the scene at least twice. Talk about the student comments in turn. Talk about the scene as a whole.
- Note how the 'You should's build up the tension. Grandad responds to Sandy's 'You should come down the café' with 'You should just get on with the dishes.' Instead of accepting the riposte, Sandy tops it with 'And you should think about helping a bit'. That leaves Grandad with the more defensive 'never been spoken to like that'. Even then Sandy comes back with a response and Grandad is left with the appeal to another authority – 'your father'.
- Remember that the washing up has been waiting since breakfast. Is Grandad so ill that he is unable even to do that? Has he sounded that ill?

3 Supported practice

- Ensure that everyone gets started. Move around to encourage and help with their ideas.
- Draw class attention to any common problems that are emerging. If one group is working much better than others, show the class what they are doing.

4 Independent work

- One minute is a reasonable target for most student scenes.
- Encourage pairs to get the endings right. Getting a row going is the easy bit!

5 Securing the skills

- Concentrate on evaluating whether the characters are convincing and whether the scenes have a discernible structure.
- Point out that drama, like story, has openings, developments and conclusions. The narrative structure matters in nearly all literary forms.

5.3 Understanding characters

Objectives S&L15, S&L16, S&L19

1 Making links

- Introduce the ideas of monologue/dialogue. Explain that when characters are alone on stage, they often let the audience into secrets: what they have done or how they are feeling. You are allowed 'inside the head' of the character.

1 Make the possible connection between Grandad not being in his own home and not being in the best frame of mind.

- Make clear the tension created by the front room having two uses.
- Make the parallel between Grandad being displaced from his normal environment and Sandy from normal routines and rights in his/her own home.

2 Whole class

Model text: Monologue by grandfather based on above play

OHT 5.1 supports this activity

1. Individuals choose two best comments; you can rank them based on student votes.
2. Give class three minutes to make individual choices. Ask each student to defend at least one adjective.
3. Ask suitable student to perform monologue, or do it yourself. Alternatively, use OHT 5.1 and highlight the words that Grandad might emphasise as he speaks. These include: *whole life, stupid, me, nothing, dead, home, might, useless.*

3 **Supported practice**

Worksheet 5.1 supports this activity

1 a) *café*; b) *Grandad*; c) *that he or she can't watch TV*; d) *stands up to Grandad*.

2 Alternatively, cut out words and give groups of three students five words each. Ask them to decide which ones they want to keep and which ones they want to swap for better ones. Give them three to four minutes to trade within their group. Find out which words people wanted to keep and which words they wanted to trade for others. Come up with a final list of four or five.

3 Use the words chosen, and let the students be Sandy for 30 seconds. If they are reluctant or unsuccessful, offer at least two versions of Sandy yourself.

4 **Independent work**

Homework sheet 5.1 supports this activity

- Establish the kinds of things Sandy might say using the script starters, getting students to complete a sentence and add a further one. When you are happy that all students have some ideas, allow independent writing. This activity can be completed as a homework assignment.

5 **Securing the skills**

- Look for the positives in each performance, e.g. *pacing of the speech; variety of tone within the speech; sense of conviction in the performance*.

5.4 Writing a script

Objectives W6, S3, Wr6, S&L16, S&L19

1 **Making links**

- Link how Grandad behaved (rudely, dismissively, sarcastically, argumentatively) to what happens generally when people are in bad moods.

2 **Whole class**

Model text: annotated script of family argument

Worksheet 5.2 supports this activity

- Reinforce these key features for writing script by hand: *speaker's name on left; speaker's name in capitals; stage directions underlined; stage directions in brackets*. Use of different coloured inks can support these features.
- When a script is printed, **bold type** is used for people's names in the margin and stage directions are written in *italics*.

3 **Supported practice**

- Students work in pairs to invent dialogue; offer support /suggestions to pairs who are struggling. Remind students that this is drama, not biography: things that are true to life, not writing up life itself.

4 **Independent work**

Worksheet 5.2 supports this activity

- Monitor paired checking and re-drafting. Stress that neatness is only one kind of revision. Finding the right phrases and giving helpful stage directions are equally important. Use Worksheet 5.2 as support if work is sent home to be completed.

5 **Securing the skills**

- Give time to hear each other's work, perhaps spread across several lessons as 10–15 minute sessions. Consider wall display or loose-leaf book of finished work.

Understanding characters

Student Book
Unit 5 • page 50

miserable	cheerful	calm
patient	difficult	understanding
puzzled	tired	angry
friendly	ratty	bad-tempered
aggressive	angry	overworked

Worksheet

5.2

Student Book
Unit 5 • pages 52–53

How to set out a playscript

Use this page to help you with activity 2 and 4 on page 52.

When you are setting out a handwritten script:

- put the speaker's name on the left
- write the speaker's name in CAPITALS in the margin
- underline stage directions
- put short stage directions in brackets ( ).

The scene is the living room. Mum is picking up magazines.

MUM	It's always a mess.
ME	(coming in) Evening, mum.
MUM	You're late.
ME	Ten minutes.
MUM	You're always late.
ME	Not always.
MUM	(raising her voice) Don't argue with me!

Remember! In a printed script:

- **bold type** is used for people's names in the left hand margin
- stage directions are written in *italics* instead of using underlining.

Understanding characters

Student Book
5 • pages 48–49

Grandad's speech

It's all right for Sandy: there's a whole life still to be lived. What have I got left? A couple of years in front of a television being bored silly by stupid repeats. That's if I'm lucky. I didn't ask to come here. They just shoved me out of the hospital and into their car. No one consulted me. The doctors talked to my daughter, they even talked to my son-in-law, but they told me nothing. For all I know I could be dead in two weeks. Not that anyone would care. They just get on with running their blasted café and leave me here like a piece of furniture nobody needs any more.

I wanted to go home. So what if I couldn't cope? At least I'd be in a mess in my own place. Here, I'm not in a mess, I *am* the mess. I'm taking up a room they need, I'm taking up time they haven't got and I'm making it worse every time I speak.

I don't expect people to understand. I thought I might get a bit of respect but that doesn't happen these days. If you're old, you're useless. Past your sell-by date and ready to be dumped in the bin.

Homework

5.1 Sandy's monologue

Student Book
Unit 5 • pages 50–51

Name

Use this sheet to help you write Sandy's monologue.

What you have to do

1 Remember that Sandy:

- works hard in the family's café
- argues with Grandad, who has come to stay
- thinks it is unfair not to be able to watch the TV show as arranged earlier
- watches the TV in the room where Grandad is staying
- stands up to Grandad.

2 Use some of these sentence starters to help you write a speech that shows how Sandy feels and thinks.

Sandy: I know he doesn't mean to be difficult but he drives me …

Sandy: It was all right until he came. Mum, Dad and me were getting on fine. The café was going OK. We were one happy family. Then he …

Sandy: If it wasn't such hard work at the café, I think we'd all get along …

Sandy: I like him really. I try my best to cheer him up. It's just that …

Sandy: The problem's having him in the front room. It used to be a place to relax. Now he's taken over ...

Sandy: I work. He doesn't. Even if he's ill, he could do a bit. Instead he …

Staging scripts – how did I do?

Name	

Think about the work you have done on staging scripts.

Tick the boxes to show what you can do.

In this unit:	I found this easy	I could do this with some help	I found this very difficult. I need to get better at this
1 I understood the characters we studied.			
2 I acted with a partner.			
3 I acted on my own.			
4 I was able to say what I thought of the drama we produced.			
5 I wrote my own playscript.			

I was best at ______________________________

I need to improve ______________________________

I will do this by ______________________________

Signed ______________________________

____

6 Choosing words for poetry

Student Book pages 54–65

Support for this unit
- Worksheets 6.1–6.3
- Homework sheets 6.1–6.2
- Self-assessment sheet
- CD-ROM activities

Teaching and learning focus
- Exploring language choices
- Experimenting with language
- Writing poetry

Objectives covered

Word level
- 14 Word meaning in context
- 15 Dictionary and thesaurus

Text level – Reading
- 14 Language choices

Text level – Writing
- 8 Visual and sound effects

6.1 Writing descriptions

Objectives W14, R14, Wr8

1 Making links
- Have your own favourite short poem ready. If students claim not to have contact with poetry, point out that they enjoy song lyrics. Rap and country music, for example, lay major emphasis upon lyrical content, albeit in very different ways.

2 Whole class

Model text: *The Thingy* by Lindsay MacRae
- Read the poem as a class. Draw attention to the key term box on alliteration.

1 Ask why a particular line is a favourite: *sound of a word, picture created in mind, etc.*
2 The animal is a dog.
3 Give students two minutes to come up with their own two-word descriptions. Work up descriptions on OHP or whiteboard/blackboard. Examples to contribute: *sea swisher; river wanderer; grass slitherer; slim hisser; hole dweller; tiny terror*. Relax the two-word limit on the descriptions if necessary.

3 Supported practice

Worksheet 6.1 supports this activity
- Get each student to write down their choices and to put them in what they think is the best order. Students can be given the words on card or paper to rearrange until the best order is achieved. Head teacher's own two-word descriptions were: *Number checker; Trouble tracker; Cheque signer; Tough talker; Parent pleaser.*

4 Independent work

Worksheet 6.2 supports this activity
- Seek quiet independent work as students make up two-word descriptions. Accept variations in the second word of the phrases if they are coming up with ideas. Try some yourself to encourage them, e.g. *Dickens reader; Rugby watcher; Coffee drinker; Calorie counter*. Worksheet 6.2 offers words that could be used.

5 Securing the skills
- Write up the best suggestions on OHP/whiteboard. Make a 'best of the class ideas' version if time allows.

6.2 Looking at rhymes

Objectives R14, Wr8

Homework sheets 6.1 and 6.2 support this section

1 **Making links**

- Make brainstorm brief. Look for full rhyme examples: *cat, mat, hat, spat.*

2 **Whole class**

Model text: *The Thingy* by Lindsay MacRae, lines 1–6

- Read the first six lines of the poem again as a class. Note rhymes that spell and sound alike first. Ask if they can think of any more. They can add to the rhymes given or be different.
- Offer an example that does not end in *-er* – 'stay' has plenty of rhymes. See how many they can suggest. If half rhymes – wrecker, kicker, tracker – are suggested, explain; leave alone otherwise.
- Address rhymes that are spelt differently. Explain that some languages, e.g. Welsh, are phonetic – how you say a word is how you spell it. English words with the same sound are spelt differently because words have come from many different countries over the centuries.

3 **Supported practice**

- This will probably require rough drafting followed by a fair copy. Answers are: *Secret sharer / Gossip bearer; Toast griller / Time filler; Final winner / New beginner; Money stealer / Biggest squealer; Head teacher / Strange creature; Mice muncher / Crisp cruncher; Playground fighter / Story writer; Second rater / Soccer hater; Best liar / Worst trier; Mud flicker / Nose picker.*

4 **Independent work**

Worksheet 6.3 supports this activity

- Get students to write their rhyme quickly without worrying too much. They can then go back, revise and edit. They can write about themselves if they wish. As this is fiction, they could create a person based on bits of several people they know.
- Prepare some couplets about yourself to show your willingness to have a go, e.g. *coffee guzzler, crossword puzzler.*

5 **Securing the skills**

- Share the poems. If possible, make a wall display. Keep a 'best of' example for future years' reference.

6.3 Choosing and using words carefully

Objectives W14, W15, R14, Wr8

1 **Making links**

- Start ideas for sound words rolling by suggesting, e.g. *the crinkle of a chocolate wrapper; birdsong; slam of the front door; dad snoring; gulls squawking.*
- Model using a thesaurus to support this activity.

2 **Whole class**

Model text 'It was ...' by Pie Corbett

1 Insist on complete silence for listening, eyes closed, perhaps heads on desks. Read the poem aloud to the class. Let students write sound words individually for one minute, then share them on OHP etc. Discuss the annotations around the poem.

2, 3 Read poem a second time. After a period of silence, brainstorm ideas on Super Power hearing: physically possible – *the swish of the grass as the ants march through* - or entirely imaginary – *the tapping of my guilty conscience when I've stolen the last biscuit.*

3 **Supported practice**

- Allow 5–10 minutes for this paired work. Circulate to help those getting stuck. Get those struggling to: 1 Choose a sound; 2 Agree what goes with the sound; 3 Agree where you would hear that; 4 Write it up into a two-line verse. They will manage it with someone at their side. Get them to do the next one unaided.

4

Independent work

- Watch for those who panic when faced with doing this on their own. Use the process described in the previous section to get them started again.
- Encourage speed followed by revision rather than agonising over every word. Encourage students with lots of material to use only the best lines.

5

Securing the skills

1 Note where the best work is before starting this section. Get at least one couplet from as many students as possible. Read out the best overall pieces.

2 The class poem could be added to the display or placed in a book of best class work.

Worksheet
6.1

Shin kicker

Student Book
Unit 6 • page 56

Parent	tracker
Number	talker
Trouble	signer
Tough	checker
Cheque	pleaser

Worksheet
6.2

Describe yourself

Student Book
Unit 6 • page 57

Describe yourself using two-word descriptions. Choose a word from box A to complete each description in B. Add your own words if you can come up with better ideas.

A

Massive	Brilliant	Fame
Great	Big	Film
Crazy	Peace	Sweet
Mad	Comic	Chocolate
Bad	Vegetable	Ace
Careful	TV	Dream
Greedy	Deep	Cola
Hopeless	Girl	Sun
Tidy	Boy	Day

Me!

I am a …

_____________ **looker**

_____________ **drinker**

_____________ **reader**

_____________ **watcher**

_____________ **eater**

_____________ **fighter**

_____________ **footballer**

_____________ **dreamer**

_____________ **hater**

_____________ **thinker.**

Worksheet
6.3

Writing a rhyme

Student Book 6 • pages 60–61

Write rhyming phrases about someone you know or have made up.

1 Choose a pair of rhyming words from box **B**.

2 Find a word in box **A** to go before each of the words. You might like to think of a word of your own. The first pair have been done for you.

A	B
big	crusher
brave	blusher
bone	stranger
house	changer
brain	drinker
word	stinker
hope	smuggler
ball	struggler
test	wrecker
sum	checker
book	mangler
time	strangler
champion	killer
chocolate	filler
work	tripper
lesson	slipper
ball	thriller
game	driller
joke	flipper
top	skipper
best	fixer
mud	mixer
leg	guzzler
hair	puzzler
music	fighter
teeth	writer
heart	winner
	spinner
	bodger
	dodger
	chaser
	racer

1 Bone crusher

Big blusher

2 ______________________

____

3 ______________________

____

4 ______________________

____

5 ______________________

____

6 ______________________

____

7 ______________________

____

8 ______________________

____

Homework
6.1

Student Book
Unit 6 • pages 58–61

Rhyme it

Name

What you have to do

Find the rhyming pairs on this sheet.

- There are fifteen rhyming pairs. Join each pair with a line.
- There are also three words that don't rhyme.

Show how good you are by getting all fifteen pairs.

date	pick	start
trouble	top	filler
shake	hate	rhyme
sign	love	pet
book	killer	house
danger	pop	type
rough	stick	mine
part	write	make
cook	bet	drink
mouse	pipe	stranger
stuff	time	fight

Rhyme it: homework answer sheet

Check your answers. How many did you get right?

1	date	hate
2	pick	stick
3	start	part
4	top	pop
5	filler	killer
6	shake	make
7	rhyme	time
8	sign	mine
9	pet	bet
10	book	cook
11	house	mouse
12	danger	stranger
13	type	pipe
14	rough	stuff
15	write	fight

These words don't rhyme with any of the others:

trouble	love	drink

Self-assessment

6

Student Book
Unit 6

Poetry – how did I do?

Name	

Think about the work you have done on poetry.

Tick the boxes to show what you can do.

In this unit:	I found this easy	I could do this with some help	I found this very difficult. I need to get better at this
1 I used two-word phrases to describe myself.			
2 I learned how to use rhymes.			
3 I used words from a thesaurus.			
4 I wrote my own poem about sounds.			

I was best at ____________________

I need to improve ____________________

I will do this by ____________________

Signed ____________________

____

7 Exploring setting and mood

Student Book pages 66–77

Support for this unit
- Worksheets 7.1–7.3
- OHT sheet 7.1
- Homework sheet 7.1
- Self-assessment sheet
- CD-ROM activities

Teaching and learning focus
- Understanding descriptions of settings (inference and deduction)
- Writing descriptions of settings
- Understanding evocative descriptions
- Understanding and writing descriptions of mood

Objectives covered

Text level – Reading
- 8 Infer and deduce
- 12 Character, setting and mood
- 14 Language choices

Text level – Writing
- 1 Drafting process (drafting)
- 14 Evocative description

7.1 Understanding descriptions of setting

Objectives R8, R12

1 **Making links**

1, 2 Students brainstorm the sorts of things a writer can tell readers about to show what these places are like: **1**) a market; **2**) busy part of a city. In preparation for their own writing it is useful if students are encouraged to brainstorm sights, sounds, smells, things you can touch, taste, etc.

2 **Whole class**

Model text: Extract from *Face* by Benjamin Zephaniah

OHT 7.1 supports this activity

1 Use the text describing East London to demonstrate how to pick out clues and infer and deduce what the place is like.

2 Students discuss what the second sentence of the model text tells readers, such as: *it's loud, it's very hot, people who live in that area like loud music and convertible cars.*

3 **Supported practice**

Worksheet 7.1 supports this activity

- The reading level of this text may be quite high for some students, in which case read the text with them first before they read it more closely for this task. Alternatively do this whole task with them and treat **4** as supported practice.

1, 2 In pairs, students study highlighted clues in the next part of the text, filling in a chart as they work out what the clues suggest: *1 Lots of police sirens around; 2 The sirens are heard here – sometimes the trouble or crime is here; 3 People around this place tonight don't want to get involved in any trouble – not nosy – they are innocent. It's someone else's problem; 4 'Even the police...' shows just how relaxed tonight was – everyone is really relaxed; 5 It's so hot the police have their windows down and sleeves rolled up and radios loud – rather like the people who live there with their cars converted and music blaring out in the earlier part of the passage.*

4 **Independent work**

Worksheet 7.2 supports this activity

- Students again work in pairs. This time they pick out five clues as well as work out what they suggest. They can use the chart on Worksheet 7.2 to note down their ideas.

5

Securing the skills

1 Students share and discuss the clues they picked out and their responses to them.

2 Students explain to each other the meaning of the key term 'setting' given earlier.

7.2

Describing a setting

Objectives Wr1, Wr14

1

Making links

1 Students use a picture of a fish and chip shop to help them brainstorm things that can be seen, heard, smelt, tasted and touched in a fish and chip shop. Model making notes using a spider diagram.

2

Whole class

Model text: Drafting sentences to improve description

- Use the example given to model drafting sentences to turn them into better descriptions.

1 Help students to choose the best sentence and to explain their choice.

3

Supported practice

1 Students work in pairs to draft sentences that describe what they might hear in a fish and chip shop, using vocabulary provided.

4

Independent work

1, 2 Students work alone to write a story setting, building on their sentences from **3**. You may want to suggest that they are writing for someone from another country who has never been in a fish and chip shop, to encourage thorough describing and imaginative word use.

5

Securing the skills

1, 2 Students explain how they drafted their sentences and the choices they made.

7.3

Understanding mood

Objectives R12, R14

1

Making links

1 Prompt students to talk about places they have been to which were creepy, sad or exciting. Be prepared to start the discussion with an example of your own.

2 Ask individual students with interesting suggestions to describe their places to the class.

2

Whole class

Model text: Extract from *Kensuke's Kingdom* by Michael Morpurgo showing change of mood

1 Use the annotated model text to demonstrate how a writer's choice of words can create mood. Discuss with the class the meanings of words and their effect in a text using the reading technique they practised in 7.1. Take the opportunity for dictionary practice if words are unfamiliar to the whole class.

2 Model using a chart to note down the class's ideas.

3

Supported practice

- Students work in pairs to search for words and sentences from the rest of the text that make the mood unhappy. **1** Words: *creeping misery, argue, niggly.* **2** Two actions: *not speaking with his wife, stopped fixing things, stays away from home, just sits flicking through magazines, doesn't talk.* **3** Shorter sentence: *'Sometimes I'd come home and they just wouldn't be speaking'; 'He was scarcely ever home anyway'.*

4 **Independent work**

Worksheet 7.3 supports this activity

- Students work alone to write five sentences that explain how the examples they picked out of the text build an unhappy mood. This is an opportunity for teachers to discuss writing about texts with level 3 students, e.g. using quotation marks; making a point about the text they pick out.

5 **Securing the skills**

1 Students work as a class, sharing the examples from the text they chose and their comments about each example.
2 Support students as they explain the key term 'mood'.

7.4 Creating a mood

Objectives Wr1, Wr14

1 **Making links**

- This section encourages students to use the skills they worked on earlier to build an evocative description. Students work as a class to:
  1 Identify the mood in a piece of text (*happy*) and discuss how the words the writer chose have created it: *enjoyed, bright, happy crackle*.
  2 Recall the meaning of key terms they will need in this section: *mood* and *setting*.
  3 Say how many sentences are in the extract (*one*).
  4 Share what they already know about writing in sentences. This is an opportunity to recall the strategy taught in Unit 1.

2 **Whole class**

Model text: Descriptive paragraph about firework night

- Use the example to model writing compound sentences, following the three-step method. Use all three connectives.

3 **Supported practice**

- Students work in pairs to complete sentence starters, and use connectives to write descriptive compound sentences that keep the mood happy. Make sure that 'and' is not used for every pair.
  1 Students work in pairs to complete two short descriptive sentences.
  2 The two students then choose a suitable connective; *but*, *and*, *or*, *and* is the combination that uses all three connectives. This may need some teacher support.
  3 Both students write out the sentence they have made.

4 **Independent work**

Homework sheet 7.1 supports this activity

- Students work alone to write three more compound sentences using phrases provided.

5 **Securing the skills**

- Students share their descriptions. Listeners pick out sentences that work well and explain why.

Worksheet

7.1

Student Book
Unit 7 • page 67

Understanding descriptions of setting

Work in pairs.

1 Look at the underlined clues 1–5 in the text below. What do they suggest about East London?

2 Note your ideas in the chart below.

> Every fifteen minutes or so sirens could be [1] heard in the distance – and some not so distant [2].
>
> People took it for granted that whatever was going down had nothing to do with them [3]. All they had to do was get out of the way and stay composed as they did so.
>
> Even the police looked relaxed tonight: [4] those that were on the cruise had their windows down, shirtsleeves up and radios blasting out [5] – police radio that is, talk radio.

Taken from *Face* by Benjamin Zephaniah

Clue	We definitely know	We can reasonably guess
1		
2		
3		
4		
5		

Worksheet
7.2

Student Book
Unit 7 • page 68

Understanding setting

Work in pairs to find out what the market is like.

1 Read the text below.

2 Pick out *five* clues that tell you what the place is like.

3 Explain what each clue suggests.

4 Make a note of your answers in the chart below.

The market

The market where Dad works is all jumbly and untidy and that makes it exciting. And you never quite know what you are going to find. There's everything there – old books, masks and jokes, toys, cheeses, fish, jewellery, hats – and of course my dad with his clocks and watches. The stall holders aren't in uniform either, like they are in the supermarket. They wear what they like. In winter they're all bundled up in coats and scarves or layers of jerseys because it can get very cold in the market. That's because the roof's made of glass. You can look up and see clouds floating by and pigeons looking down at you. Anyway the *feeling* in the market isn't cold. It's warm and friendly and comforting.

Taken from *Minders* by Diana Hendry

Clue	We definitely know	We can reasonably guess
1	The market is jumbly and untidy.	A busy place with lots of different kinds of people and things.
2	You never know what you are going to find.	
3		
4		
5		

Worksheet
7.3

Student Book
Unit 7 • page 74

Understanding mood

The mood is unhappy because the writer used the (*word/action/sentence*)

____

which suggests ______________________________________

The writer used the (*word/action/sentence*) ________________________

____

which suggests ______________________________________

____

The writer used the (*word/action/sentence*) ________________________

____

which suggests ______________________________________

____

The writer used the (*word/action/sentence*) ________________________

____

which suggests ______________________________________

____

The writer used the (*word/action/sentence*) ________________________

____

which suggests ______________________________________

____

OHT

7.1 Understanding setting

Student Book
Unit 7 • page 67

East London

A

> It was a hot sticky night and East London was alive. Every car stereo was turned to the full, every convertible car was converted and every house that had a fan was burning up electricity.

Taken from *Face* by Benjamin Zephaniah

definitely know	**can reasonably guess**
East London	
hot sticky night	*it's summer*
alive	*it's a busy area*

Writing longer sentences

Student Book
Unit 7 • page 76

Name

What you have to do

1 **Finish the *five* sentences below.**

2 **Read your sentences. Tick each one that:**
- makes sense – if it doesn't, then rewrite it
- begins with a capital letter
- ends with a full stop.

1 The fireworks were great fun but ____________________

____________________ ☐

2 One of the rockets fell over and ____________________

____________________ ☐

3 ____________________

____________________ but it had set fire to some paper. ☐

4 ____________________

____________________ or they would have had to dial 999. ☐

5 A man took some photographs of the fire and ____________________

____________________ ☐

Exploring setting and mood – how did I do?

Name	

Think about the work you have done on setting and mood.

Tick the boxes to show what you are able to do.

In this unit:	I found this easy	I could do this with some help	I found this very difficult. I need to get better at this
1 I found words which showed what a place was like.			
2 I improved sentences to make them better descriptions.			
3 I explained what **setting** means.			
4 I picked out words which made the mood unhappy.			
5 I wrote longer sentences.			

I was best at ______________________________

I need to improve ______________________________

I will do this by ______________________________

Signed ______________________________

____

8 Exploring an older poem

Student Book pages 78–87

Support for this unit
- Worksheets 8.1–8.3
- OHT sheet 8.1
- Homework sheet 8.1
- Self-assessment sheet
- CD-ROM activities

Teaching and learning focus
- Studying a poem from a different time
- Seeing how form and meaning work together
- Understanding a poem's significance

Objectives covered

Word level
- 16 Unfamiliar words

Text level – Reading
- 1 Locate information
- 14 Language choices
- 19 Poetic form
- 20 Literary heritage

Speaking and Listening
- 10 Report main points
- 11 Range of roles
- 12 Exploratory talk
- 13 Collaboration

8.1 What makes a ballad?

Objectives R1, R14, R19, R20, S&L13

1

Making links

1 Be prepared to recall the words of your own favourite song as a start. Direct students towards song genres that often use narrative – country and rap, for example. Consider having an example on tape or CD to play.

2 Read the explanation box about ballads with the class. You might like to draw a comparison with playground songs that change as they pass from generation to generation of children.

2

Whole class

Model text: *How comes that blood?*

OHT 8.1 has a copy of the poem to support work on this activity and throughout this section

- Read the poem aloud and then read the poem again. Answer the questions.

1 '*How comes that blood all over your shirt?*'

2 *'It's the blood of my little guinea pig'.*

3 *Blood of hunting dog, blood of old roan horse.*

4 *Killed his brother.*

5 *He's planning to run away to sea.*

3

Supported practice

Worksheet 8.1 provides tables for student answers in this activity

- Allow students to offer more than one example for each of the things found in ballads, if they wish. Each student should make their own copy of the table. Suggested answers are: Repeated lines: *My son, come tell it to me; It's the blood of ...* Words at the end of lines that rhyme: *me/sea.* Questions and answers: *How comes that blood all over your shirt? ... It's the blood of my little brother Bill; And what will you do when your father comes home? ... I'll put my feet in the bottom of a boat/And sail across the sea.*

4 **Independent work**

- Answers suggested are as follows.

1 About families: *line 2: my son; line 4: mother; line 15: my little brother Bill; line 17: your father.*

2 About death: *line 3: about his guinea pig; line 11: about his horse; line 15: about his brother.*

3 About fear: *line 4: 'O mother, please let me be.' lines 19–20: 'I'll put my feet in the bottom of a boat/And sail across the sea.'*

5 **Securing the skills**

Homework sheet 8.1 may be used at this point

1–3 Give the students who will read the poem warning and the opportunity to practise. Let several students have a go at trying some of the excuses as individual lines after the initial reading.

4 Recap points about the ballad form, mentioning that murder is the most common subject.

8.2 Why we read older poems

Objectives W16, R19, R20

1 **Making links**

- Get a volunteer to tell the story of 'How comes that blood?' Do not interrupt for corrections. Let the story be told and discuss accuracy at the end.

1 *'Yonder' has become 'over there' in standard English. The nearest to 'How comes' today would be 'How come', or a variant of 'How the ____ have you ...'.*

2 *Arguments, questioning and murder are all part of this ballad, and still fill the newspapers.*

3 Explore what students now expect a ballad to be like.

2 **Whole class**

Model text: Poem about Nathan's trainers based on 'How comes that blood?'

1 Two of the lines will fit into the verse about Nathan's trainers. The third – *My brain won't work* – will not scan. If students suggest it, read it aloud: it sounds wrong.

2 This verse has: *the question and answer format; words that rhyme; argument.*

3 **Supported practice**

Worksheet 8.2 supports this activity

- Get students to write out lines, cut them up and move them around until they are satisfied with the verse, then paste it up.

4 **Independent work**

Worksheet 8.2 supports this activity

1 Ask students to repeat individually the process above to create the first verse.

2 Students complete two lines and find an excuse for the third line of the second verse.

5 **Securing the skills**

Worksheet 8.3 supports this activity

- Compare versions. Come up with a favourite final version. If time allows, make up further verses in the same pattern. An example is given on Worksheet 8.3. Identify the ballad features it contains.

8.3 Developing good ideas

Objectives S&L10, S&L11, S&L12, S&L13

1 **Making links**

1 Talk about practical suggestions that make talking in groups easier for everyone involved. Let students choose from the suggestions provided. Reinforce any established class rules about group work.

2 Excuses; most will have understood that, but you could explain about text and sub text.

2 **Whole class**

Model: Possible excuses for use in a performed conversation

- The key purpose of this activity is to generate ideas. Go over the question and the answers given. Get as many further excuses as fast as you can. Ideas from real life are usually offered first, but encourage some creative fiction as well. Write up as many as you have space for. Repeat the process for parental replies.

3 **Supported practice**

- Insist on a few minutes of silent work to make individual decisions about which are the best excuses. Allow a further three/four minutes to debate the merits of the three excuses given.

4 **Independent work**

1 Groups should remain the same for this section. Help groups assign the individual roles for this activity. While students are working together, they are also carrying an individual responsibility, so getting the best fit is important.

2 Groups will get stuck if they try to take the whole thing at one bite. Get them to take it a bullet point at a time and help accordingly. If some groups struggle, use a successful group in a 'goldfish bowl': they go through what they have been doing in the centre of the room whilst the others sit around the outside and observe.

3 Make sure that the students read the points for each crew member before performing their stories. The teacher may want to go through these points with the class.

5 **Securing the skills**

1 One good point from each 'director' and one point for improvement should be a minimum contribution.

2 Consider turning ideas about group talk into a class charter, e.g.:
   - Everyone has a right to be heard.
   - You must listen to what others say.
   - You must speak in turn.
   - Each person in a group has an equal voice.
   - No one should be made fun of for speaking up.

Worksheet
8.1

What makes a ballad?

Student Book
Unit 8 • page 79

Things you often find in ballads	Example
Repeated lines	
Words that rhyme at the ends of lines	
Questions and answers	

Things you often find in ballads	Example
Repeated lines	
Words that rhyme at the ends of lines	
Questions and answers	

Worksheet
8.2

Student Book
Unit 8 • pages 83–84

Writing your own ballad

Gary knows what happened,

Nathan, just tell me how.

That's all I can say for now.

I ate three buttons for my lunch,

How come you've ripped your new school shirt?

And wouldn't let it go.

The dog was playing catch with me

How come you've lost your English book?

Nathan, I need to know.

How come you've lost your tie again?

________________ *what's going on?*

____

So it isn't ________________ *that's wrong.*

Writing your own ballad

Compare your ballad with the one below. It was written by some Year 7 students.

Nathan's trainers

How come you've trashed your new trainers?
Nathan, explain that to me.
They sent us running in the rain,
So it's not my fault, you see.

How come you've ripped your new school shirt?
Nathan, just tell me how.
Gary knows what happened,
That's all I can say for now.

How come you've lost your English book?
Nathan, I need to know.
The dog was playing catch with me
And wouldn't let it go.

How come you've lost your tie again?
Nathan, what's going on?
I ate it 'cause I had no lunch
So it isn't me that's wrong.

OHT
8.1 How comes that blood?

Student Book
Unit 8 • pages 78–81

"How comes that blood all over your shirt?
My son, come tell it to me."
"It's the blood of my little guinea pig –
O mother, please let me be."

"Your guinea pig's blood is not so red.
My son, come tell it to me."
"It's the blood of my little hunting dog
That played in the field for me..."

"Your dog lies yonder, O my son,
And this it could not be."
"It is the blood of my old roan horse
That pulled the plough for me..."

"How comes that blood all over your shirt?
My son, you must tell to me."
"It's the blood of my little brother Bill
Who I killed in the field today..."

"And what will you do when your father comes home?
My son, come tell it to me."
"I'll put my feet in the bottom of a boat
And sail across the sea."

Homework

8.1

The best excuses

Student Book
Unit 8 • page 79

Name

What you have to do

Show how good you are at making excuses! Complete each sentence below with the best excuse you can think of.

1 A good excuse for getting home late would be ______________________

____

2 A good excuse for being late to school would be ______________________

____

3 A good excuse for not doing my homework would be ______________________

____

4 I might get out of work at home by saying ______________________

____

5 The excuse that never seems to work with teachers is ______________________

____

6 An excuse that didn't work at home was ______________________

____

7 If I broke a large window and got sent to the deputy head's room, my excuse would be ______________________

____

____

____

____

____

Exploring an older poem – how did I do?

Name	

Think about the work you have done on an older poem.

Tick the boxes to show what you are able to do.

In this unit:	I found this easy	I could do this with some help	I found this very difficult. I need to get better at this
1 I understood what ballads are.			
2 I found out what sorts of things you may find in a ballad.			
3 I helped to put together our own ballad.			
4 I took part in discussions.			
5 I worked with others to play a scene.			

I was best at ______________________________

I need to improve ______________________________

I will do this by ______________________________

Signed ______________________________

____

9 Recounting events

Student Book pages 88–97

Support for this unit
- Worksheets 9.1–9.3
- OHT sheet 9.1
- Homework sheet 9.1
- Self-assessment sheet
- CD-ROM activities

Teaching and learning focus
- Recounting events
- Speaking and writing formally and informally
- Playing different roles

Objectives covered

Word level
- 20 Connectives

Sentence level
- 4 Tense management
- 5 Active or passive voice
- 6 Resolve ambiguity
- 13b Recount
- 15 Vary formality
- 16 Speech and writing
- 17 Standard English

Text level – Writing
- 10 Organise texts appropriately

Speaking and Listening
- 17 Extend spoken repertoire

9.1 Recounting a scary event

Objectives W20, S4, S13b, Wr10

1 **Making links**
- Encourage students to recount two or three events from the most recent episode of their favourite soap opera. Question, using temporal link words: *What happened next?* Help students to talk about events in chronological order. Ask the name of the text type they are speaking: *recount*. Elicit what they can remember about recounts from Key Stage 2.

2 **Whole class support**

Model text: Spoken recount text
- Read the text aloud, twice if necessary. Ask students what kind of text it is and what makes this a recount.
- Ask students to identify past tense verbs. Perhaps make a list on the board or OHT. Ask what past tense verbs tell you about when events happened.
- Ask students to identify time link words. Students will have used the term 'connective' for time link words in Key Stage 2. Again, list these words on the board.
- **Extension** – ask students to add any other time link words they know to the list.

3 **Supported practice**
1. Pairs of students predict what might happen when Arif got back to school. Ask how they are going to decide on the order of the sentences: *by looking at time link words: D, B, F, E, A, C.*
2. Model recounting a scary event using past tense verbs and time link words. Ask students to think for a minute about an event to recount. Students recount to a partner.
- Feed back to students good uses of time link words and the past tense, i.e variety or consistency of time link words; past tense used consistently and appropriately.

4 **Independent work**

Worksheet 9.1 offers further practice in these skills
1. Remind the students of their event, then model how to write three sentences using past tense words and time link words. Students then write their own sentences.
2. Students reinforce their understanding of the past tense and time link words by underlining examples in their work.

5 **Securing the skills**

- Encourage students to identify the key features of a recount: *verbs in past tense, use of temporal connectives.*

9.2 Formal and informal English

Objectives W20, S4, S15, S17, S&L17

1 **Making links**

- Allow students to recap, e.g. write time link words and a sentence using the past tense on individual whiteboards, then showing you the whiteboards all together.

2 **Whole class**

Model text: Examples of an informal and formal recount

OHT 9.1 supports this activity

- Read the first recount using an informal tone; establish that the students have understood what has happened. Ask how they know that this is a recount, and for an example of the past tense and a time link word. Then read the second text with a more formal tone and ask for an example of the past tense and a time link word. Ask how the two versions are different. Help them by asking what difference it makes who they are speaking to, or why Josh wouldn't talk to the Head of Year in the same way as to his friend. Introduce the terms 'formal' and 'informal'.
- In the first text, underline 'you know', 'kids' and 'stuff' on the OHT. Explain that these informal words are used when talking to friends and family. As a class, underline the other informal words and phrases: *'you could hear a pin drop'; 'went off'; 'I went all hot'; 'Boy, was she in for a surprise!'; 'screamed blue murder'; 'in trouble with a capital T'*. Point out that informal spoken recounts tend to be embellished.

3 **Supported practice**

- The teacher may want to do an example orally to check understanding of the task.
- A pair of confident students could perhaps be asked to demonstrate how the role play should work. After the role play, ask a pair to perform to the class, who pick out the aspects of formal or informal English. If the pair get some parts wrong, they could 're-play' using the class's suggestions.

4 **Independent work**

- Ask students to finish the sentences in their books.

5 **Securing the skills**

- Check the sentences orally. Lead a class discussion on the difference between formal and informal English, ensuring that every student is clear about the distinction.

9.3 Writing formal English

Objectives S5, S15, S17

1 **Making links**

- Recap here the differences between formal and informal English using the questions provided. Ask students to give you examples when they are explaining. Use some of the words and phrases from 9.2 to remind the students if necessary.

2 **Whole class**

Model text: Incident form

Worksheet 9.2 supports this activity

- Ask students to recount what happened with Josh in the exam hall, and if they recognise the type of form. Make links with the school's own version. Ask if they would expect formal or informal English to be used; don't confirm or disagree at this point.

1–3 Read the form through, including all the details at the top. Ask students to find the features of a recount and then tell you if it is formal or informal and to explain why.

- Point out the formal uses of language in the annotations. Point out the passive constructions and explain that this construction is used when what happens is more important that who did it. More work on this is provided on Worksheet 9.2. Ask students to find an example in the recount.

3 **Supported practice**

1, 2 Remind students of the role play they performed in 9.2. Focus attention on the recount and ask pairs to carry out the task. Take feedback, asking students to explain their decisions. Ask how they would rewrite the informal sentences in a more formal way.

4 **Independent work**

Worksheet 9.3 supports this activity

1, 2 Students rewrite informal sentences as formal ones, then fill in an incident form.

5 **Securing the skills**

- Ask students to carry out the checks. Ask what students have put in the action box. The teacher might work on examples of a passive sentence for the action box as a class.

9.4 Differences between speech and writing

Objectives S6, S16, S&L17

Homework sheet 9.1 supports this section

1 **Making links**

- The list-making activity can be done as a class on the board. If students find this difficult, say a couple of sentences with hesitation or repetition, followed by two without to make the distinction clear. Comment on formal/informal language, complete/incomplete sentences, and clarity of pronouns.

2 **Whole class**

Model text: Transcript of newspaper interview

- Establish what an interview is and the context of a newspaper journalist. Read the interview to the class. Ask confident students to read the roles.

1. Elicit answers in general terms first, then ask for evidence from the text.
2. When we speak, we think and speak almost simultaneously, so there is little time to formulate what we are saying.
3. It is not clear from the pronouns if Paul is talking about the laptop or the mobile. Confusing pronouns are quite common in speech but must be avoided in writing.

3 **Supported practice**

- The role play allows students to hear the features of spoken language in a realistic setting. Explain how the different roles work, but avoid overdemonstrating: only having to think and speak will produce the features the students are listening for. Find out to what extent each feature was present in the students' interviews.

4 **Independent work**

- Make sure students make the link between the dialogue and the reporter's interview. Model how they might go about the task and record their findings in a chart. Suggest that they list what the reporter has taken out, e.g. *most of the questions*.

5 **Securing the skills**

- Ask students to feed back their lists. Build up a class list to consolidate the learning.

Recounts and time link words

Student Book
Unit 9 • page 89

1 Write a time link word or phrase in each gap. Choose from the box below. Remember to use a capital letter if the time link word is at the beginning of a sentence.

Last week, I went shopping with my mum. It was so boring.
______________, she dragged me into her favourite clothes shop.
______________, I had to wait while she tried on tons of clothes.
______________, she asked which clothes looked good on her. We
______________ went to a department store – we visited every department!
______________ we went for lunch. In the afternoon we visited more clothes shops. ______________, at five o'clock, she asked me if I wanted to look at anything. I was so tired I said no!

finally   then   first   after that   next   later

2 Read this recount. There are two sentences missing in the middle. Write two sentences that fit. Use time link words or phrases.

Polly went to a football match last weekend. Her school was playing the school down the road. At first, the match was very slow. At half time, nobody had scored a goal.

In the second half, it was much better. Then, a player from the other team was sent off! Now Polly's team could win!

____

____

____

____

Polly shouted with joy – two goals scored with only ten players. Finally the whistle blew. Polly's team had won.

Worksheet

9.2

Active and passive verbs

Student Book
Unit 9 • page 93

Explanation

These sentences contain **passive** verbs:

Josh ***was sent*** to the Head of Year for behaving badly.

In science, the Bunsen burner ***is used***.

Use passive verbs when *what is being done* is more important than *who does it*.

1 Choose the correct word to write in the gap.

a The meat ______________ (is / were) cooked in a medium oven for two hours.

b The house ______________ (is / was) broken into last night.

c The liquid is then ______________ (pours / poured) into a beaker and ________ (is / was) heated on the Bunsen burner.

d Applications for this job will be ______________ (accepted / accept) until 30th November.

2 Change these active sentences into passive sentences. The first one has been done for you.

a Last week, someone discovered a new star in the Milky Way.

Last week, a new star was discovered in the Milky Way.

b Someone cancelled the football match yesterday.

____

c Someone found a kitten in the street.

____

d Someone will light the bonfire at seven o'clock.

____

Worksheet
9.3

Writing formal English

Student Book
Unit 9 • page 94

Write your recount of what happened in the library here. You may need to make up some information. Remember to use:

- formal English
- time link words
- capital letters and full stops.

Dawson Comprehensive School

Incident form

Date of incident: ____________________

Place of incident: ____________________

Person reporting incident: ____________________

Pupil(s) involved in incident: ____________________

Brief recount of incident: ____________________

____

____

____

____

____

____

____

Action: ____________________

____

____

OHT

9.1 Formal and informal English

Student Book
Jnit 9 • page 91

Josh was talking to a friend. This is what he said:

I was taking my maths test, you know, in the big hall. All the kids' bags and stuff were at the front of the hall. At first, you could hear a pin drop. Then a mobile phone went off, it was dead loud. I went all hot – it was mine! Next the teacher began hunting in the bags. Finally, she got to mine. Boy, was she in for a surprise! My pet mouse was in a box in my bag. Next, she screamed blue murder as my mouse ran up her arm! In the end, everyone laughed so much the test had to stop. Later, I got into trouble with a capital T.

Then Josh talked to his Head of Year. This is what he said:

I was taking my maths test. All the students' bags were at the front of the hall. At first, all the students worked in silence. Then my mobile phone rang really loudly. Next, the teacher tried to find the phone to turn it off. I knew what she would find. Then she found my bag and screamed when she opened it. My pet mouse was in a box in my bag. In the end, the test had to be stopped. I am very sorry.

Answer these questions.

1 These two are both recounts. How do you know?

2 How are the two versions different?

Writing a newspaper report

Name

What you have to do

1 **Read the interview A below.**

2 **Read the beginning of the report B that appeared in the local newspaper. Finish it using formal English.**

A

The local newspaper interviewed the head teacher of Dawson Comprehensive School. She was interviewed about how a group of students made a robot and won a competition.

Reporter: Tell me about the robot idea.

Head teacher: What do you mean, how we came to make it?

Reporter: Yes.

Head teacher: Well, let me think ... er ... yes it was the D&T teacher, Ms Carpenter, she heard about it and thought it would be a good idea.

Reporter: How did you decide who would make the robot?

Head teacher: Year 8, or was it Year 9? Yes, it was Year 8 – they needed a new project. So they made this fantastic robot, I mean, really fantastic robot made of metal and it can move very fast . So the teacher entered the robot in the competition and we won – it was great. The students are over the moon.

Reporter: Thank you.

B

Students Win Robot Competition!

Students in Year 8 at Dawson Comprehensive School recently won a competition with a model robot. The D&T teacher, Ms Carpenter, wanted a new project for the year group.

____

____

____

____

____

____

Student Book
Unit 9

Recounting events – how did I do?

Name

Think about the work you have done about recounting events, speaking and writing both informally and formally.

Tick the boxes to show what you are able to do.

In this unit:	I found this easy	I could do this with some help	I found this very difficult. I need to get better at this
1 I recounted events using time link words (*first, then,* etc.).			
2 I spoke informally in role play.			
3 I spoke formally in role play.			
4 I wrote formally on an incident form.			
5 I looked at the differences between speaking and writing.			

I was best at ______________________________

I need to improve ______________________________

I will do this by ______________________________

Signed ______________________________

____

10 Finding information

Student Book pages 98–107

Support for this unit
- Worksheets 10.1–10.2
- OHT sheets 10.1–10.2
- Homework sheet 10.1
- Self-assessment sheet
- CD-ROM activities

Teaching and learning focus
- Locating information
- Identifying main points in paragraphs
- Using reading strategies such as highlighting/underlining to extract information
- Comparing ways in which information is presented
- Using suitable planning format such as spider diagram
- Selecting and presenting information

Objectives covered

Sentence level
- 9 Main point of paragraph

Text level – Reading
- 1 Locate information
- 2 Extract information
- 3 Compare presentations
- 4 Note making

Speaking and Listening
- 1 Clarify through talk
- 7 Pertinent questions

10.1 Where to look for information

Objectives R1, R3, S&L1, S&L7

1 **Making links**

OHT 10.1 supports this section and provides an* aide memoire *for activity 4

- Write up on the OHT sheet provided as many additional sources of information as you can in two or three minutes. Here are some further suggestions: *textbooks, neighbours, television, older brothers/sisters, magazines, other relatives, newspapers, older pupils you know, encyclopaedias, shop assistants.*

2 **Whole class**

Model text: Enquiry questions

- Concentrate on the pros and cons of different information sources. The Internet and Gran are extremes of what is available. The Internet provides vast quantities of information but a student would have to know what they were looking for. In contrast, a person offers very specific memories but ones that reflect what happened in their life during that period.
- The flooding question allows you to contrast what is available in local and national newspapers. The other obvious source of information would be someone who had experienced the flood or who lived close by. A secondary source would be someone who had been told of what had happened although they were not there themselves. The quality of information/evidence is dealt with in detail in history and there is potential for cross-curricular linkage here.

3 **Supported practice**

1 Suggested answers: **a)** Thomas Edison: *encyclopaedias, Internet, library books, science textbooks.* **b)** Roald Dahl: *Internet, library books.* **c)** Wildlife programmes: *TV listing magazines.* **d)** India: *library books, CD-ROMs, encyclopaedias, Internet.* **e)** Electric fires: *catalogues, other relatives, shop assistants.*

4 **Independent work**

Use OHT 10.1 on screen with ideas generated in activity 1

1 The things the students want to find out can be for personal interest or because of current homework/teacher requirements. Only offer ideas as a last resort.

2 Get students to list as many places/people where information might come from as possible. The sorts of questions to be raised here are: *What sources of information might be available for this? Which are realistically accessible? Which are most reliable? Which are easiest to use?* ***Who*** *might help me as well as* ***what*** *might help me?* Where answers to questions are accessible, they can be sought (possibly through homework), but the key issue here is the process, understanding how you go about finding things.

5 **Securing the skills**

Homework sheet 10.1 can be used throughout this unit; this is an appropriate point

- Use the questions from **4** as a checklist for the discussion. Seek agreement on best sources for each item you want to find out, but recognise that different students have different learning styles.

10.2 Finding information in a book

Objectives R1, R2, R3, S&L7

1 **Making links**

- Find out about *Matilda* via the contents or the index. Most people tend to look at a contents page first, although it is usually quicker to use the alphabetical index. There is no shame in admitting that you start by just flipping through the book. Plenty of adults do just that, but it simply isn't the most efficient method. Possible answers: *look at a summary of his life – a timeline, for example; find* ***M*** *in index; find a chapter on the subject.*

2 **Whole class**

Model text: Contents list and index from book about Roald Dahl

- Look at the annotations together. Stress the process of scanning, i.e. not reading every word closely, but searching for the words you actually need and ignoring the others. Some people use fingers, some use rulers, some simply use their eyes and nothing else – it is worth trying different ways. Reinforce what you are doing by having at least one non-fiction book in class. Answers to questions: **1** *p49 and p64;* **2** *pp7–15;* **3** *True;* **4** *What happened when, a chronology.*

3 **Supported practice**

- Suggested answers: **A** *Chapter 6*; **B** *first job;* **C** *Chapter 9*; **D** *father;* **E** *9 and 57.*

4 **Independent work**

- Answers to quiz: **A** *True*; **B** *False*; **C** *False*; **D** *True*; **E** *True*.

5 **Securing the skills**

1 Give students time to say what they have learned. Ask what, if anything, they find difficult about finding what they want in a book.

2, 3 Contents gives you a view of the whole book; Index lets you get into the detail. An index is normally more useful than a contents list, but the size of an index and the need to scan alphabetically put people off. Stress that the effort pays off.

10.3 Making notes

Objectives S9, R1, R2, R3, R4

1 **Making links**

1, 2 Get student ideas on how to remember information. The task can be set as a ten-minute homework before the lesson. Possible memory techniques may include: *reading over and over what you have to remember; reading it and getting someone to ask you questions about it; finding the key points; finding a way to visualise what you have to remember.* The last two require good note-making. As students often have a horror of the phrase 'making notes', emphasise that this is actually about making learning easier.

2

Whole class

Model text: Paragraph about spiders and student notes

Worksheet 10.1 supports this section (use first as an OHT)

- Just reading paragraphs is not the best way to learn about a topic. Make sure students are clear about the terms being introduced. Reinforce where necessary, both here and later in the section. Stress that we are asking: What is really important?
- Stress the need for legibility when creating notes. If you can't read them, you can't use them.

3

Supported practice

Worksheet 10.1 supports this activity

1 Try to ensure that both students in each pair contribute. One can suggest the first two answers, the other the second two, with each checking the other. Suggested answers: *a) webs; b) thick liquid; c) two holes at the back; d) thin line.*

2 Notes could read like this: *Making webs; silk inside – liquid; comes out two holes – back; in air →thin line.*

4

Independent work

Worksheets 10.1, 10.2 and OHT 10.2 support this activity

- Stress the need to plan the use of the page when setting out a spider diagram. The work here will be challenging for many students, so support those who are struggling.

5

Securing the skills

- Students who do well will have discovered how they can remember things best. Remember that different students have different strengths: auditory; visual; kinaesthetic. The first two have most use in schools but all three can be used fully across a lifetime. One thing remains constant: the more you use your memory, the better it will become.

Worksheet
10.1

Spiders

Student Book
Unit 10
pages 103–107

Use the text below to help you with activities 2, 3 and 4.

Everyone knows what spiders look like, but what do we know about them? They are not insects. Insects have six legs. Spiders have eight legs. They belong to a family of animals called arachnids.

Spiders are best known for spinning silk webs. The silk comes from inside the spider and it starts off as a thick liquid. The silk can be squeezed out of two holes in the back of the body. The moment that the liquid hits the air, it dries into a thin line.

One of the biggest spiders in the world is called the tarantula. It can grow to a length of 25 centimetres. It normally only comes out at night and can catch frogs and snakes as well as insects. Tarantulas are unusual because they are furry.

Spiders like to eat insects alive or just after they have killed them. They have fangs in their mouths and poison glands in their jaws. They use the fangs to inject poison into the insects they have caught. Then it's lunchtime!

Worksheet
10.2 Spider diagram

Student Book
Unit 10
◆ pages 106–107

Use this diagram with activity 4.

OHT
10.1

Sources of information

Student Book
Unit 10
◆ pages 98–99

Places	People
radio	teachers
library books	classmates
CD-ROMs	parents
Internet	experts you know

OHT
10.2 Answer sheet

Student Book
Unit 10
◆ pages 106–107

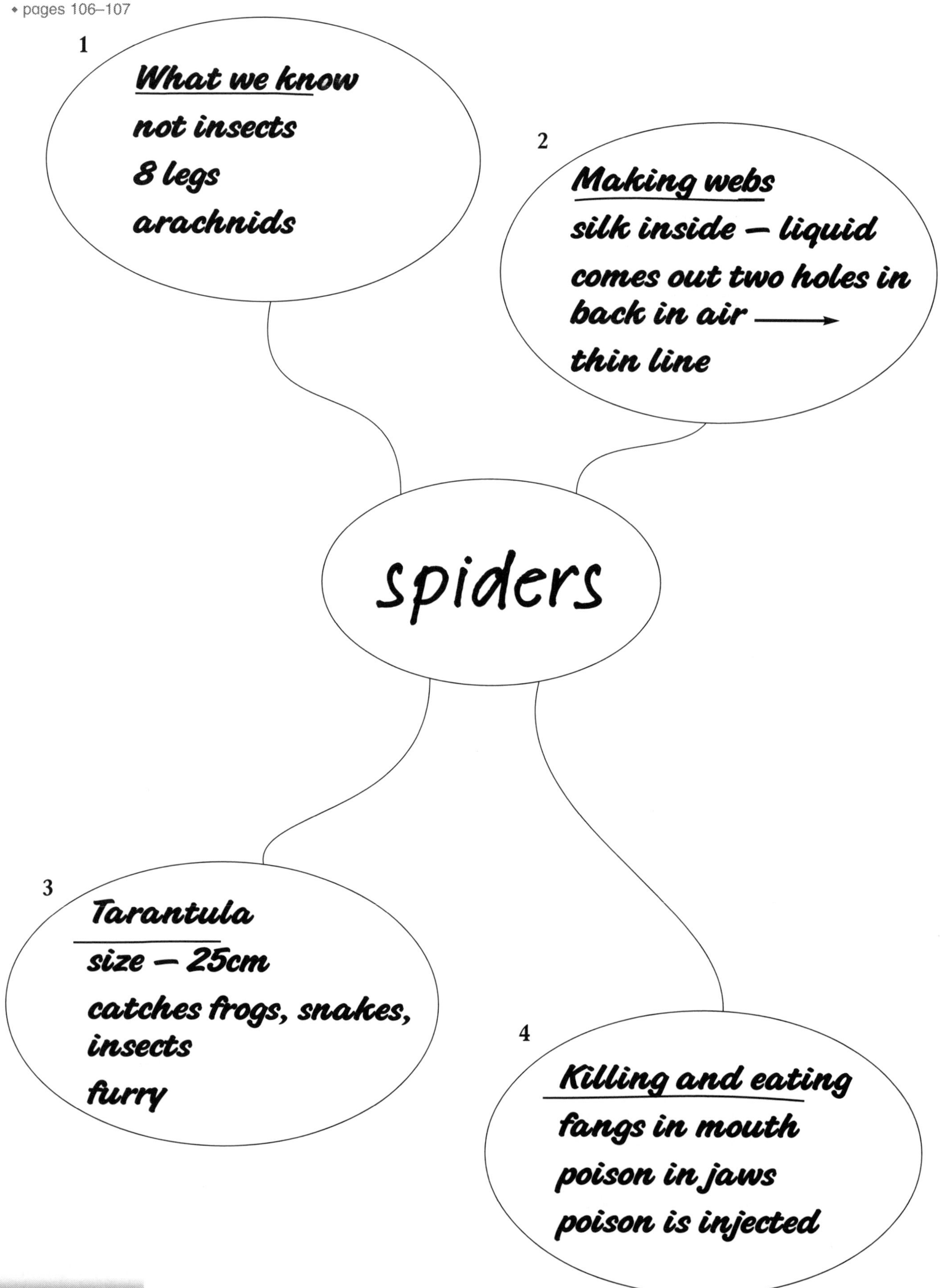

Homework

10.1

Student Book
Unit 10

Information hunter

Name	

What you have to do

Are you a top information hunter? See how you do in the big info hunt!

Answer the questions on this sheet.

1 Name *three* television programmes you could be watching at 7.30pm on Friday.

a ______________________________

b ______________________________

c ______________________________

2 Name the favourite television programmes of *three* people not in your class.

a ______________________________

b ______________________________

c ______________________________

3 Look at a newspaper. Write down *three* things it gives you information about.

a ______________________________

b ______________________________

c ______________________________

4 Name *three* ways you could find information if you needed it.

a ______________________________

b ______________________________

c ______________________________

Finding information – how did I do?

Name	

Think about the work you have done on finding information.

Tick the boxes that show what you can do.

In this unit:	I found this easy	I could do this with some help	I found this very difficult. I need to get better at this
1 I learned where to find information.			
2 I used a contents page.			
3 I used an index.			
4 I found the main point in a paragraph.			
5 I found key points in a text.			
6 I made notes.			

I was best at ______________________

I need to improve ______________________

I will do this by ______________________

Signed ______________________

____

11

Presenting information

Student Book pages 108–113

Support for this unit
- Worksheet 11.1
- OHT sheets 11.1–11.2
- Homework sheet 11.1
- Self-assessment sheet
- CD-ROM activities

Teaching and learning focus
- Planning and drafting text
- Revising and presenting text
- Putting ideas into suitable format

Objectives covered

Sentence level
- 13a Information

Text level – Reading
- 5 Evaluate sources
- 13 Non-fiction style

Text level – Writing
- 1 Drafting process
- 2 Planning formats
- 4 Handwriting and presentation
- 11 Present information
- 12 Develop logic

11.1

Who are you writing for?

Objectives R5, R13, Wr1, Wr11, Wr12

1 **Making links**
- Get as many ideas as you can about where to find information. Ideas should include: *places, written sources, people*. Include obvious things like notice boards.

2 **Whole class**

Model text: Alternative opening paragraphs for school leaflet
- Discuss the openings. None is wrong, but only **B** targets parents in language with which they will be comfortable. A school leaflet shouldn't sound like a radio advertisement, and vice versa. Make sure all students write down opening **B**.
- Leaflets for new pupils and their parents have a twofold purpose. They are written primarily to inform, but also to reassure the newcomers.

3 **Supported practice**
- Pairs of students repeat the process in **2**. Remind both students in each pair to write down the sentence they have agreed is the best: **F** is the suggested option.

4 **Independent work**
- Working individually, students repeat the process, choosing more than one sentence this time. Explain that there is more than one answer here, but some sentences may seem too informal for a school leaflet. Sentence **I** is the least formal because of the phrase 'a great bunch of people'. Make sure sentences are written down. Ask students to think about the ordering of the sentences they have chosen.

5 **Securing the skills**
- Hear the students' answers. Talk about: *the formality of the introduction; the order of the sentences*. If students are having difficulties with the concept of formality, put together the most informal sentences to create a contrast.

11.2 Planning and writing a leaflet 1

Objectives R5, R13, Wr1, Wr2, Wr4, Wr11

1 **Making links**

- If details about information that you need on a first day arose earlier, recap this. Focus here on the specific requirements of the first day. Students don't need everything on Day One, but they do need the essentials. What are they?

2 **Whole class**

Model text: Outline of school leaflet

OHT 11.1 supports this activity

- Number one priority is *space*. If everything is crammed together, nothing stands out and usually very little gets read. Another issue is *size*: the address of the school is important but the name is even more important. *Headings* help to break up the text and send readers to the relevant part of the text. *Positioning:* not everyone will bother to read the whole leaflet, so make sure that important information is on the front. The 'Who to contact' issue is addressed below, but share ideas to start students off.

3 **Supported practice**

1 The people on the 'Who to Contact' list should not simply be a hierarchy of the school, but the people who readers might need to speak to, e.g. the education welfare officer, but not the head of sixth form. You will inevitably need to provide the spelling of some names, so be prepared.

2 Students should know times of the school day but may need help with lesson times.

3 Remind students that this leaflet cannot cover every single detail and that selection is just as important as accuracy.

4 **Independent work**

- Put OHT 11.1 back up on screen as a reminder of what is required. Circulate early in the process of writing up the front page of the leaflet in order to pick up those who have got the layout seriously wrong and need to start again. It is frustrating to get three-quarters of the way through and find your design will not work. Get students to review neatness and legibility as they work. Ask how they think they can improve in these areas.
- Keep the best front pages from year to year to help those who struggle with layout. Don't let them copy slavishly but do let them see what others have done.

5 **Securing the skills**

- The purpose of this activity is to give credit where credit is due and to highlight good practice. Offer praise not just for the neatest but for those who exemplify the principles of leaflet layout: *good spacing; clear headings; design that is easy to follow.* Brainstorm what they have learned so far about planning and writing an information text: *formality of language, sequence, layout,* etc.

11.3 Planning and writing a leaflet 2

Objectives S13a, Wr1, Wr2, Wr4, Wr11

1 **Making links**

1, 2 A list of your school's clubs/activities and a copy of the school rules would be useful here. Remember that the aim is not to reproduce every school rule but to provide a good summary of what new pupils need to know.

2

Whole class

Model text: Page from a school leaflet

OHT 11.2 supports this activity

Homework sheet 11.1 offers practice with imperatives

- Put OHT 11.2 on screen. Stress again the importance of headings and layout.
- Talk about where bullet points might be used rather than continuous prose: *for lists; where phrases are being used rather than full sentences; where several points are being made one after another.*
- Explain imperatives and give further examples. Show how imperatives differ from statement sentences.

1 Get students to make their own lists of activities. Remind them that the range of activities on the leaflet should appeal to all kinds of students.

2 Students do not have to agree on the most important rules for the school. Get them to write rules in their own words. Check that they are using imperatives.

3

Supported practice

- Get pairs talking about what to do when ill. Once they can agree, get one to dictate the answer while the other writes. Repeat process with roles reversed for what to do when late. Make sure that both students make copies of the answer they dictated so that each has a full set of information.

4

Independent work

Worksheet 11.1 extends this activity

- Put OHT 11.2 on screen again as a prompt. Remind students of the work they did on the front page of the leaflet. Reinforce previous advice about spacing and use of headings. Stress that good planning saves time and frustration later. Circulate early to pick up those who have got the layout wrong and may need to start again. Get students to suggest improvements in presentation.
- Keep back best pages from year to year as exemplars for those who struggle with layout.
- ***Extension***: Students use Worksheet 11.1 to produce a copy of the school rules for display.

5

Securing the skills

1 As a class, look at each leaflet in turn and discuss whether it is more suitable for parents or for students. Factors include: *language level*; *content*; *legibility*; *level of detail.*

2 Highlight those who exemplify the principles of leaflet layout: good spacing, clear headings, designs that are easy to follow. Give credit for whatever good practice you observe. The best of these leaflets can be shown to the person responsible for new pupils at your school.

3 Factors that make an information text easy to read: *layout, spacing, headings, neatness of presentation, use of language, omitting unnecessary detail, font size*, etc.

- Recap on the terms encountered in this unit: *audience, purpose, layout, heading.*

Worksheet
11.1

School rules

Student Book
Unit 11
◆ pages 112–113

School Rules

1 ______________________________

____

____

2 ______________________________

____

____

3 ______________________________

____

____

4 ______________________________

____

____

OHT

11.1 School leaflet 1

Student Book
Unit 11
pages 110–111

Rushford High School

Lower Market Street,
Rushford, NH23 8YU
Telephone: 01669 7541 3321

Introduction

Who to Contact

Times of the School Day

OHT
11.2

School leaflet 2

Student Book
Unit 11
◆ pages 112–113

Activities

Here are some of the things you can do and take part in here:

- ◇ ______________________
- ◇ Reading Buddies
- ◇ ______________________
- ◇ Resource Centre
- ◇ ______________________
- ◇ ______________________
- ◇ Trips to ______________
- ◇ ______________________

School Rules

- ◇ Listen carefully to ______________________
- ◇ Make sure you ______________________
- ◇ Wear ______________________
- ◇ Walk ______________________

Lateness

If you are late, you need to ______________________

____

Illness

If you are ill, please ______________________

____

Homework
11

Student Book
Unit 11 • page 112

Do it like this

Name

What you have to do

1 Read these examples:

You are doing it like this. a **statement**

Do it like this. an **imperative** or command

2 Turn the statements below into imperatives.

1 You need to eat your dinner.

Ea ______________________________

2 You should clean up the mess in your bedroom.

C ______________________________

3 You ought to help with the washing up.

____

4 You could take the dog for a walk.

____

5 I hope you're going to stop picking your nose.

____

6 It is time to start writing now.

____

7 This letter needs to be posted.

____

Presenting information – how did I do?

Name	

Think about the work you have done on presenting information.

Tick the boxes to show what you can do.

In this unit:	I found this easy	I could do this with some help	I found this very difficult. I need to get better at this
1 I chose the right language for a leaflet.			
2 I understood the need to write for my audience.			
3 I collected useful information together.			
4 I organised my information.			
5 I used headings.			
6 I set out my work clearly.			

I was best at ______________________________

I need to improve ______________________________

I will do this by ______________________________

Signed ______________________________

____

12 Explaining things carefully

Student Book pages 114–127

Support for this unit
- Worksheets 12.1–12.2
- OHT sheet 12.1
- Homework sheet 12.1
- Self-assessment sheet
- CD-ROM activities

Teaching and learning focus
- Giving a spoken explanation
- Discovering how explanation texts are organised
- Seeing how points are linked in paragraphs
- Explaining a process in a series of paragraphs

Objectives covered

Word level
- 20 Connectives

Sentence level
- 9 Main point of paragraph
- 12 Sequencing paragraphs
- 13c Explanation

Text level – Reading
- 7 Identify main ideas

Text level – Writing
- 2 Planning formats
- 11 Present information
- 12 Develop logic

Speaking and Listening
- 1 Clarify through talk
- 4 Answers, instructions, explanations
- 7 Pertinent questions

12.1 Asking questions and answering them

Objectives S&L1, S&L4, S&L7

1 **Making links**
- Students list words you can use to begin questions: *who, what, how, when, why, where, which.* You could also discuss other ways of forming questions, e.g. *beginning with verbs such as did/does, would, should, could, is,* etc.

2 **Whole class**

Model: Picture of office after theft for students to answer questions

1 Demonstrate how to make sense of a detailed picture by searching the picture, asking questions and making links between different information. Introduce and emphasise the need for link words in explanations: *because, so (that), since, therefore, as, when,* etc.

2 Students work out that the wallet containing £40 has been stolen through reading the head teacher's speech bubble and looking at the open and empty drawer.

3 **Supported practice**
- Students study the picture and work out explanations to answer the five questions. As they present their answers, reinforce the idea of varying link words, otherwise 'because' will be used for every answer, e.g. *The drawer was forced open when the thief searched for the wallet.*

4 **Independent work**

Worksheet 12.1 supports this activity. Photocopy and cut up sufficient copies for each pair of students to have their own pictures and instructions.
- Pairs of students work in role, one as Robert, the other as Mr Tait. They use different pictures. Mr Tait asks Robert about his appearance because he looks suspicious. Robert bases his answers on a picture showing him being asked to work in a garden.

5 **Securing the skills**

1 The class works out explanations of why Mr Tait thinks Robert is the thief using pictures **A** and **B**. The discussion should include: *Robert's torn trousers – perhaps torn on the broken glass as he climbed in or out of the office; His shopping cost £40 – the exact amount stolen in the wallet; Robert's muddy shoes – the thief left muddy footprints; His hand is cut but no longer bleeding – he could have done it when breaking the window.*

2 Asking questions made students think about what they were seeing. It helped them work out what had happened/how to explain things.

3 Students showed their ideas were sensible by explaining why they thought what they did and using evidence from the picture.

4 Students used the picture like this: *searched the picture, asked questions about what they saw, searched for other linked information, pointed to it when explaining.*

12.2 Reading an explanation text

Objectives S9, S13c, R7

Homework sheet 12.1 supports this work

You might prefer to photocopy a suitable page from an explanation text for students to read rather than letting them select their own.

1 **Making links**

1 a) What the text is explaining: *how a lie detector works*. b) What the text will tell you: The discussion should include: *What a lie detector is, How it works, Why it is used.*

2 Students are asked to read the text and discover where different information is given. Discuss different reading strategies, e.g. scanning to gain an overview of what the text is about and where information is located, before reading the text more closely. a) paragraph A; b) paragraph B; c) paragraph C.

3 Students share what they already know about paragraphs: *they show the writer is going to write about a new place, person, time, idea; each new paragraph is begun on a new line.*

2 **Whole class**

Model text: Text explaining how a lie detector works

OHT 12.1 supports this activity

- Explain and demonstrate how to: **1** find the main point of a paragraph; **2** work out what the smaller points are doing; **3** identify link words.

3 **Supported practice**

1 The correct sequence is: C, D, A, B.

2 The linking words are: *however, because.*

4 **Independent work**

1 The main point: *The lie detector is linked to a set of machines.*

2 One smaller point – any of the other sentences.

3 One linking word: *meanwhile; at the same time* is a linking phrase.

5 **Securing the skills**

1 *What ...? How ...? Why ...?*

2 True – explanation texts should be written in paragraphs.

3 Smaller points tell readers more about the main point. Main points tell readers what the paragraph is about.

4 Any four link words.

5 *Verb phrases in an explanation are often in the present tense.*

12.3 Planning an explanation

Objectives S12, S13c, Wr2, Wr11, Wr12

1

Making links

1 Recap the different functions of main points and smaller points in paragraphs.

2 An explanation text says: ***what*** *happens,* ***why*** *it happens,* ***how*** *it happens.* Also recap other features of explanation texts, e.g. *often in the present tense, paragraphs.*

2

Whole class / Supported practice

N.B. There is no independent work in this section.

Model text: Chart for planning explanation text

Worksheet 12.2 supports this section

- Students follow a series of steps to plan an explanation text. Model the technique for each step before students attempt to complete their plans. A completed chart might look like this (numbers are included to help with step 4 – the order of the points):

Paragraph	Main points: What happens	Smaller points: Why it happens	Smaller points: How it happens
Paragraph 1: introduction	[1] The person tells a lie	[2] The truth will get them into trouble. [3] They don't want to get in trouble.	[4] The brain thinks of something to say – not the truth: 'it wasn't me!'
Paragraph 2	[5] The brain sends a message to the rest of the body.	[6] The brain knows that the body needs to get ready to run away or fight.	[7] The brain releases chemicals that tell the different parts of the body what to do.
Paragraph 3	[8]The heart starts to pump blood round the body faster.	[9] The heart beats more quickly.	[10] The heart muscle works harder.
Paragraph 4	[11] The lungs send more oxygen round the body.	[12] The lungs start to breathe faster.	[13] The chest moves in and out more quickly.
Paragraph 5	[14] The hands and feet start to sweat more.	[15] The body has got hotter and needs to cool down.	[16] When the blood takes the energy from the liver it gets hotter.
Paragraph 6: conclusion	[17] A lot happens when you tell a lie. Telling the truth is a lot easier!		

3

Securing the skills

- Four things to do when planning an explanation text: *1 Decide what you are explaining; 2 Make a list of the main points; 3 Decide what smaller points support each main point; 4 Decide in what order to write about all the points.*

12.4 Linking points together

Objectives W20, S13c

1

Making links

1 Students share what they already know about when to start a new paragraph and how to begin a new paragraph *(with a main point).*

2 Students work alone to sort link words into three groups – those they know and use, those they know but don't use, words they don't know. They can then look up words they don't know in a dictionary.

3 Students work as a class to complete sentences which use the more sophisticated link words. This activity can also be done as a game which checks and builds students' understanding of all the link words.

Sentence Glue

1 Divide students into two or more teams.
2 Write part of a sentence that begins or ends with one of the link words.
3 All the students have to try to finish the sentence so it makes sense, e.g. *The person is in trouble* **so** *they tell a lie.*
4 The first person to finish the sentence wins a point for the team. Continue until all the link words have been used.

2

Whole class

Model text: Two points to link together

- Use the example to demonstrate choosing the link word to join points together to explain something.

1 Links can be made using: *as, since, so, therefore.*

3

Supported practice

- Students work in pairs to suggest link words missing from a text. Possible answers: *Then; so/therefore; Next; Therefore; since/because.*

4

Independent work

- Students write a paragraph of the explanation text using link words.

5

Securing the skills

- Students mark each other's paragraphs, underlining link words and ticking each sentence that makes sense. This is an opportunity for whole class discussion of students' paragraphs and ways of improving them through the choice of link words.

Robert's explanation

Student Book
Unit 12
◆ pages 116–117

Mr Tait

Look at the picture below. Ask Robert five questions about what he looks like, and what he has been doing.

1 *How did you rip your trousers?*

2 *Where were you ...*

____

____

3 ________________________________

____

4 ________________________________

____

5 ________________________________

____

Robert

Look at the picture below. Work out an answer to each question you are asked by Mr Tait:

1 *Mr Tait: How did you rip your trousers?*

Robert: I tore them on some brambles.

2 *Mr Tait: Where were you* ____________

Robert: ________________________

____

3 *Mr Tait:* ________________________

Robert: ________________________

4 *Mr Tait:* ________________________

Robert: ________________________

5 *Mr Tait:* ________________________

Robert: ________________________

Worksheet
12.2

Planning an explanation

Student Book
Unit 12
◆ pages 122–124

Paragraph	Main points:	Smaller points:	Smaller points:
Paragraph 1: introduction	• the person tells a lie	• truth will get them into trouble • don't want to get in trouble	• brain thinks of something to say – not the truth: 'it wasn't me!'
Paragraph 2	• the brain sends ____	• brain knows ____	____
Paragraph 3	• the heart ____	____	____
Paragraph 4	• the lungs ____	____	____
Paragraph 5	• the hands ____	____	____
Paragraph 6: Conclusion	• a lot happens when you tell a lie ____	____	____

OHT
12.1 Main points in paragraphs

Student Book
t 12 • page 120

Find out how paragraphs are written.

1 Read the paragraph below and its labels. Then answer the question below.

Main point — First an interviewer asks the person wearing the lie detector a question.

Smaller points — Then the person says their answer. Meanwhile the interviewer is checking what the lie detector is showing.

> First an interviewer asks the person wearing the lie detector a question. Then the person says their answer. Meanwhile the interviewer is checking what the lie detector is showing. Sometimes people tell lies. However, the interviewer knows if an answer is a lie because the lie detector shows the person speaking is stressed.

2 What is the difference between main points and smaller points?

The main point ______________________________

____

____

____

The smaller points ______________________________

____

____

____

Homework
12.1 Reading an explanation text

Student Book
Unit 12
• pages 118–121

Name ____________________

What you have to do
1 Find an explanation in another book. You could choose a text book from geography, history or science, or a library book.   **2 Read the explanation carefully. Answer the questions below.**

1 What is the book's title (on the front cover)?

____

2 Who wrote the book?

____

3 Find a page where something is being explained. Read it carefully and fill in the chart below.

Questions	Answers
1 What is explained?	What ____________________ ____________________ How ____________________ ____________________ Why ____________________
2 What do any pictures show the reader?	____________________ ____________________ ____________________
3 Choose one paragraph. Copy out the main point of the paragraph.	____________________ ____________________ ____________________
4 Make a list of any link words the writer has used in the paragraph.	____________________ ____________________ ____________________

Explaining things carefully – how did I do?

Name

Think about the work you have done on explaining things.

Tick the boxes to show what you are able to do.

In this unit:	I found this easy	I could do this with some help	I found this very difficult. I need to get better at this
1 I used talk to work out what had happened in Mr Tait's room.			
2 I gave a spoken explanation using a picture.			
3 I found the main ideas in a text.			
4 I found the main point in a paragraph.			
5 I worked out how the rest of the paragraph added to the main point.			
6 I planned a series of paragraphs.			
7 I used link words in my writing.			
8 I wrote a paragraph of explanation text.			

I was best at ______________________

I need to improve ______________________

I will do this by ______________________

Signed ______________________

13 Giving instructions

Student Book pages 128–131

Support for this unit
- Worksheet 13.1
- OHT sheet 13.1
- Homework sheet 13.1
- Self-assessment sheet
- CD-ROM activities

Teaching and learning focus
- Giving spoken instructions
- Writing instructions
- Ordering instructions using link words

Objectives covered
Word level
- 20 Connectives

Sentence level
- 13d Instructions

Text level – Writing
- 13 Instructions and directions

Speaking and Listening
- 9 Oral text types

13.1 Giving spoken instructions

Objectives W20, S&L9

1 Making links

- Ask pupils to look at the two sentences on their own for two or three minutes. If they cannot see which is the good instruction, ask them to think about which they *have* to do and which gives them the choice.

2 Whole class

Model text: Instructions given by boy for accessing the Internet

1 Point out that Joseph is giving instructions to his Gran and is using the imperative form of the verb. If necessary, point out that the imperative is made by removing the subject of the verb. Ask students to find more examples of imperative verbs.

2, 3 Ask students why time link words are used with instructions. Then ask for as many examples as they can give. They may know these as 'connectives' from KS2. Show how the instructions are sequenced using time link words.

3 Supported practice

- Ask students to tell you how to use a mobile phone. Begin with how to switch it on.
- Look at the instructions in the text book and identify the first one with the students. Ask students to complete the task. Check the order is correct: *D, A, E, C, B.*

4 Independent work

- Ask students to recap for you what a time link word or connective is. Students then complete the activity, putting in either a connective or an imperative. Ask students to check in pairs before taking feedback.

5 Securing the skills

- Model how to give spoken instructions for one of the items listed. To present more of a challenge, add in extra helpful information like: 'First you switch on the Gameboy. *Then you will see the screen appear.*' Focus on the 'you will see' to support students in adding in extra information.

13.2

Writing instructions

Objectives S13d, Wr13

Homework sheet 13.1 will prepare students for this section

1

Making links

- Ask pairs to list places where written instructions are seen; the pair with the longest list are 'winners'.
- Establish that clarity and order are important when writing instructions, as well as making sure that steps are not omitted.

2

Whole class

Model text: Simple instructions for using a video

- Ask students if anyone in their house has difficulty with understanding written instructions for electrical items or gadgets.
- Read through the instructions. Ask students to identify the imperatives. Ask the two suggested questions in the student book. Ask why numbers might be preferable to time link words in written instructions.

3

Supported practice

Worksheet 13.1 extends this activity

- Ask students to do this activity independently at first. Then they can check their work with a partner. When taking feedback, ask students *how* they arrived at the order.
- **Extension:** Worksheet 13.1 offers an exercise in sequencing instructions using time link words and a certain amount of logic. Many students may need some support with this worksheet, and teachers may prefer to use this as a class activity. The correct sequences are: Police Station: *A, E, C, B, D*; Post Office: *J, F, H, I, G*.

4

Independent work

OHT 13.1 supports this activity

- Rehearse orally with the students what they are going to write. Ask them whether they will use time link words or numbers to order the instructions.
- OHT 13.1 allows you to do some whole class writing of instructions before this stage if necessary. Demonstrate writing the instructions for the first picture; ask students to make suggestions for the second two pictures (shared writing); then ask students to complete the last two pictures independently.

5

Securing the skills

- After students have completed the checking tasks, ask them if they think their partners had good examples of instructions. If so, they should read out their partner's work and say why they think the instructions were good.

Worksheet
13.1

Student Book
Unit 13 • page 131

Instructions

Read the two sets of instructions here. There are directions to the Police Station and to the Post Office, but they are muddled up. Work out the right order. Put the letter for the right order in each box below.

Police Station

A First, walk down the road until you see the video shop on your left.

B Next, turn right at the traffic lights.

C Walk down Allen Road until you see the traffic lights.

D You will see the Police Station a little way down the road on the right.

E Then you take the first left after the video shop. This is Allen Road.

Directions to the Police Station

1	
2	
3	C
4	
5	

Post Office

F Then, after the park, take the next road on the left. This is Park Road.

G The Post Office is on the opposite corner. You can see it.

H Next, walk down Park Road. The park will still be on your left.

I At the end of Park Road, about 100 metres after the park, is a junction.

J First, walk up the road keeping the park on your left.

Directions to the Post Office

1	
2	
3	H
4	
5	

OHT
13.1

Writing instructions

Student Book
it 13 • page 131

Making biscuits from a packet

Homework

13.1 Looking at instructions

Student Book
Unit 13
• pages 130–131

Name	

What you have to do

1 **Look around your home. Find *four* examples of written instructions.**

2 **Fill in the chart below.**

Example 1	
What are the instructions for?	
Write one line of the instructions.	
Do you think the instructions are clear? Do they use numbers or time link words?	
Example 2	
What are the instructions for?	
Write one line of the instructions.	
Do you think the instructions are clear? Do they use numbers or time link words?	
Example 3	
What are the instructions for?	
Write one line of the instructions.	
Do you think the instructions are clear? Do they use numbers or time link words?	
Example 4	
What are the instructions for?	
Write one line of the instructions.	
Do you think the instructions are clear? Do they use numbers or time link words?	

13

Self-assessment

Giving instructions – how did I do?

Name	

Think about the work you have done about spoken and written instructions.

Tick the boxes to show what you are able to do.

In this unit:	I found this easy	I could do this with some help	I found this very difficult. I need to get better at this
1 I gave spoken instructions about how to use or do something.			
2 I gave written instructions on how to use or do something.			
3 I used words like 'first' and 'then' to order my instructions.			

I was best at ______________________________

I need to improve ______________________________

I will do this by ______________________________

Signed ______________________________

____

14 Offering advice

Student Book pages 132–137

Support for this unit
- Worksheet 14.1
- OHT sheets 14.1–14.2
- Homework sheet 14.1
- Self-assessment sheet
- CD-ROM activities

Teaching and learning focus
- Giving spoken and written advice
- Practising drama techniques

Objectives covered

Sentence level
- 3 Boundary punctuation

Text Level – Writing
- 10 Organise texts appropriately
- 17 Informal advice

Speaking and Listening
- 18 Exploratory drama

14.1 Giving informal advice

Objective S&L18

1 **Making links**
- Before attempting the question, make sure students understand the term 'advice'. If students find it hard to think of words used to offer advice, suggest some situations where they are likely to have been offered advice.

2 **Whole class**

Model text: Speech bubbles with advice texts
- You could ask students to read the words of Alice and her friends. Explain the need for the right intonation; model it if necessary.
- Take the students through the questions and annotations. The key point to make is that you *have* to follow instructions, but you can choose whether to follow advice.

3 **Supported practice**
- Demonstrate with a student what is required to complete the task. Recap the need for the correct intonation when offering advice. The role of offering advice can be done by both students in the pair: there are enough examples of things Pete could do. Ask a pair to show their work to the class.

4 **Independent practice**
- Demonstrate with a student what to do for the role play, using the example. You could ask the students to think of possible courses of action for the first role play to build up their confidence.

5 **Securing the skills**
- Ask as many pairs as time allows to show their role plays. Emphasise the need to be constructive when evaluating how well their peers offered advice.

14.2 Giving written advice 1

Objectives S3, Wr17

1 **Making links**

- The discussion around the questions will prepare students for the activities that follow. The questions could be answered in pairs quickly first before responding as a class. The term 'surfing' could be introduced here.

2 **Whole class**

Model text: Advice on safe surfing

OHT 14.1 supports this activity

- Read the 'Safe surfing for kids' text with the class. Establish what 'surfing' is if this wasn't done above. Question the students to check for understanding.
- Introduce the negative instruction with 'never' or 'don't'. Underline the negative instructions on the OHT or ask students to do this.
- Work through the instructions with the students to establish that the imperative is used because the situation is very serious. 'Why don't you ...' and 'You could ...' are not appropriate here.

3 **Supported practice**

- Introduce the task and ask for one or two examples.
- Take feedback. The teacher may want to insist that students use the suggested constructions.

4 **Independent practice**

- Explain the task. Focus students on the need for the leaflet to 'look' serious but appeal to teenagers. Ask students to suggest some ideas. Remind them of the audience if their suggestions are inappropriate.

5 **Securing the skills**

- Once the pairs have checked the work, examples could be read out and shown to the class. Ask the students to say how well the advice has been given and in what form. Ask for comments on the layout of the leaflet.

14.3 Giving written advice 2

Objectives S3, Wr10, Wr17

1 **Making links**

- Get the students to list quickly the ways you can give informal advice in writing. Remind them of the work from the previous section.

2 **Whole class**

Model text: Problem page letter

OHT 14.2 supports this section

- Cover up the response to Rio's letter. Read Rio's letter aloud to the class. Check students' understanding through questioning. Point out the structure of the letter – the letter begins with what the problem is and then explains why it is a problem.
- Ask students what advice they would give to Rio. Read Craig's response and check for understanding. Take students through the questions, establishing that the same constructions are used for both spoken and written informal advice. Ask students to come and underline the phrases for giving advice in Craig's response.
- Point out the punctuation at the ends of sentences: full stops and question marks.

3 **Supported practice**

Worksheet 14.1 supports this activity

- Ask students to tell you what punctuation goes at the end of each sentence.

4

Independent practice

Homework sheet 14.1 supports this activity

1 Take one of the examples and demonstrate the writing if necessary. Next, choose an example and rehearse orally what students might write. Remind students to write neatly as others will need to read their letters.

2 Swap letters around the class and draw attention to the prompts.

5

Securing the skills

- When students say who gave the best advice, ask them to refer not only to the content but also to the use of the suggested structures.

Full stops or question marks?

Student Book
Unit 14 • page 137

Read this letter. Put a full stop or a question mark in each gap.

Dear Marsha,

I am twelve years old ____ I really want to be a model ____ I've tried to think of something else but I can't ____ I am good-looking and I like clothes ____ Am I old enough to become a model yet ____ I really don't know what to do ____ Can you help me ____

Thanks,

Ally

Giving written advice

Student Book
Unit 14 • page 134

Safe surfing for kids

1 Never tell anyone online your last name, address, phone number or where you go to school. And always keep passwords secret!

2 Tell your mum/dad or teacher if anything online makes you feel uncomfortable. (If they're not there, just sign off and tell them later.)

3 Never meet up with an online friend offline, unless your mum or dad goes with you. You can never be sure that people are telling the truth about themselves.

4 Make sure you know where files are from before you download them. They could have 'viruses' that damage your computer.

5 Don't send nasty messages or chain letters. If you get any, stop reading and tell your mum or dad.

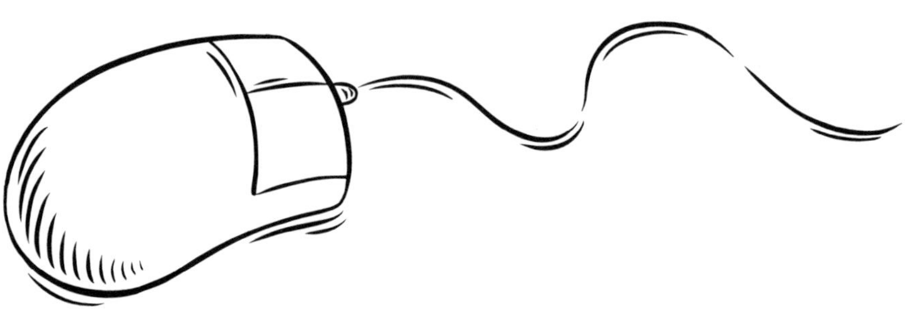

OHT
14.2

Giving written advice

Student Book
nit 14 • page 136

Read the problem page letters below.

1 List *three* different ways Craig gives advice.

2 What kinds of punctuation does he use at the ends of sentences?

Dear Craig,

I am 13 years old and I really want to be a pop star. It's all I've ever wanted to do. My parents think I am stupid. Do you think I am? They want me to be good at school. They say I should concentrate on my exams and forget my dreams. My friends say that I have a good voice. They think my voice is good enough to be famous. What should I do?

Yours,

Rio

Dear Rio,

Lots of teenagers want to be pop stars. I don't think you are stupid. Not many make it; in fact, very few become famous. Why don't you listen to your parents? They have a point. Try hard at school and get your exams. You may change your mind later and you will need qualifications. Why don't you join a local band? You could ask your friends to help you. You could also take singing lessons. This way, you will please your parents and become famous too.

Good luck!

Craig

Homework
14.1

Student Book
Unit 14 • page 137

Giving written advice

Name

What you have to do

Read this letter to a problem page. Then do the work below.

Dear Bobby,

I have a real problem. All my friends at school tease me because I have a different accent from them. I only moved here last summer. They think I don't mind. I pretend I don't, but I do. I really do. I've spoken to my mum. She just says to get tough.

Please help.

Sean

1 List the things Sean could do.

1 ______

2 ______

3 ______

2 Write a letter back to Sean giving him advice.

Dear Sean,

______

______

______

______

______

______

Offering advice – how did I do?

Student Book
Unit 14

Name	

Think about the work you have done about offering spoken and written advice.

Tick the boxes to show what you are able to do.

In this unit:	I found this easy	I could do this with some help	I found this very difficult. I need to get better at this
1 I gave spoken advice in role.			
2 I designed and wrote a leaflet giving strong advice.			
3 I wrote a letter asking for advice.			
4 I replied to someone else's letter asking for advice.			
5 I used full stops and question marks to show the ends of sentences.			

I was best at ____________________

I need to improve ____________________

I will do this by ____________________

Signed ____________________

15 Understanding the audience

Student Book pages 138–147

Support for this unit
- Worksheets 15.1–15.3
- Homework sheet 15.1
- Self-assessment sheet
- CD-ROM activities

Teaching and learning focus
- Understanding how magazine covers attract their audience
- Using a mind map to organise ideas
- Writing about a media text

Objectives covered

Text level – Reading
- 10 Media audiences
- 11 Print, sound and image

Text level – Writing
- 3 Exploratory writing
- 19 Reflective writing

Speaking and Listening
- 3 Shape a presentation
- 6 Recall main points
- 7 Pertinent questions
- 19 Evaluate presentations

15.1 Understanding media and audience

Objectives R10, Wr3

1 Making links
- Before allowing them to look in the dictionary, ask students to explain what they understand by 'audience'. Write an initial definition on the board or flipchart. Once students have checked in the dictionary, work on refining the class definition together, perhaps with an example. Record this definition for future reference.
- It is very important for students to have a clear idea of the everyday meaning of 'audience' because the media use of the term is similar but not the same.

2 Whole class

Model text: Mind map of the media a student likes
- Introduce the class to a mind map, using the annotations and information in the student book. You might wish to draw attention to the key terms box and the definition of media at the bottom of page 139.
- Ask the questions suggested in the student book. The aim is to support students' understanding of the media idea of audience: that a TV programme, advert or magazine is produced to appeal to certain groups of people. If this proves difficult, ask them about what media different members of their families like. Get them to guess what *you* like. Focus on age and gender to keep it as simple as possible.

3 Supported practice
- After the paired discussion, ask for feedback and reinforce the notion of age and gender defining to a large extent what media items people like.

4 Independent work

Worksheet 15.1 supports this activity
- Give students a clear time limit when completing the mind map about themselves. After the paired work, see how similar or different the mind maps are across the class. Ask students to account for the similarities and differences.
- ***Extension***: Collate class information into a graph to give a visual interpretation.

5 **Securing the skills**

- Finish the sentences on the board or flipchart, taking suggestions from the students. More sentences similar to, 'The audience for *The Tweenies* is ...' could be added for reinforcement. Students could record these sentences for later reference.

15.2 Who is this magazine for?

Objective R10

1 **Making links**

- Before looking at the two definitions of 'audience', ask students for a definition of the everyday meaning. The discussion allows students to distinguish clearly between the media and everyday uses of 'audience'.

2 **Whole class**

Model text: Cover of magazine *Mizz*

- Ask students which magazines they read, and if anyone reads *Mizz*.

1 Give students a few minutes to find the components of the cover. Tell them that 'image' is a media term for picture. Check for understanding of 'contents'.

2, 3 Go through the two questions, then look at the annotations. Ascertain exactly what the publishers have put on the cover to attract its audience, pre-teen girls. Make it clear that a magazine cover is designed very deliberately with its audience in mind.

3 **Supported practice**

- After the paired discussion take feedback. Make sure students give evidence for their answers from the cover and that they are not just guessing.

4 **Independent practice**

- This activity reinforces the discussion in the whole class section. The teacher may have to demonstrate how to record the information as notes.

5 **Securing the skills**

- Once students have fed back to the class, the notes could be written up into sentences. You could model how this is done. The whole class discussion should allow you to see if the difficult concept of audience has been understood.
- Remind the class of the magazines they named in **1**. Now they need to explain what attracts them to these magazines. Refer back to the components of a cover.

15.3 Writing about a magazine cover

Objectives R10, Wr19

1 **Making links**

1, 2 List free gifts on the board. Explore differences between the kinds of free gifts on girls' and boys' magazines. Explain that the free gift is carefully chosen and increases magazines sales a great deal, e.g. women's magazines often give away bags.

2 **Whole class**

Model text: Cover of *Disney's Big Time* issue 14

1, 2 Answer the questions before considering who the audience is (*mainly boys, aged 8–11*). Students should give evidence based on the cover for their suggestions. Some features will appeal to girls too, so discussion could be interesting.

3 **Supported practice**

Worksheet 15.2 supports students in this activity

- Pairs of students fill in the chart with reasons why the features on the cover appeal to its audience. These should be quite specific; avoid 'because they like it' if possible.

4 **Independent work**

- The class could compose this sentence together if preferred.

5 **Securing the skills**

Homework sheet 15.1 is designed to consolidate work so far

- Two sentences are given as an example, but you might model the next sentence and share the writing of the fourth, suggesting that three sentences are completed independently.

15.4 Know your audience

Objectives R10, R11

1 **Making links**

- Discussing what to look for on a magazine cover in the newsagent's gives students a chance to use what they have learned so far. You could describe what you would want and then ask students to think of a particular magazine that fulfils the criteria.

2 **Whole class**

Model text: Mock up of a magazine cover aimed at 12–14-year-old boys

- Explain to students that they will have to use all they have learned in the unit so far in this section. You may want to ask a few recap questions.
- Before answering the questions, ensure that students understand who the intended audience for the magazine is. Take students through the features of the cover. Make sure students give you reasons why features will grab attention or appeal.
- The section about hairstyles is designed not to appeal to the target audience, as if the publishers have made a mistake. If students don't pick this up, point it out.

3 **Supported practice**

1 The three choices are intended to be articles or features within the magazine. All choices are good as long as they are justified in terms of the target audience.

4 **Independent practice**

Worksheet 15.3 supports this activity

- Explain that students are to use their chosen article title to fill the gap on the cover. Their design has to fit in with the rest of the cover and appeal to the target audience. Ask students to discuss their ideas with a partner before drafting a design.

5 **Securing the skills**

- Before students show their designs to the class, perhaps give them a few minutes to think about what they want to say and even rehearse it with a partner.

15.5 Talking to the publisher

Objectives S&L3, S&L6, S&L7, S&L19

1 **Making the links**

- This section allows students to think again about the cover for *Kool* magazine. Remind students who the target audience is. Do this activity as a whole class on the board or flipchart.

2 **Whole class**

Model text: Notes for a discussion about the cover of *Kool*

- Explain the task of feeding back to the publisher. Explain that to give a talk, it is important to have notes to speak from. Notes should support you when you are talking, rather than reading out every word on a piece of paper.
- Show students the model and draw attention to the annotations. You could work with the class to produce the next bullet point. Ask students to continue the notes in pairs.

3 **Supported practice**

- Take quick feedback to ensure students have understood how to do the note-taking, then ask them to complete notes for things that could be improved. Monitor the students' work to ensure that they all have notes detailed enough to speak from.

4 **Independent practice**

- Make sure students have understood the activity clearly. Talk about how to make constructive criticism of their partner's talk. Model a talk if necessary.

5 **Securing the skills**

- Before listening to the talks, make sure the class know they have to listen and ask questions after each talk. Reinforce what was said earlier about constructive criticism, perhaps modelling how to do this after the first talk.

Worksheet
15.1

My media mind map

Student Book
Unit 15 • page 139

1 **Write your name in the middle.**

2 **Write your favourite media onto the mind map.**

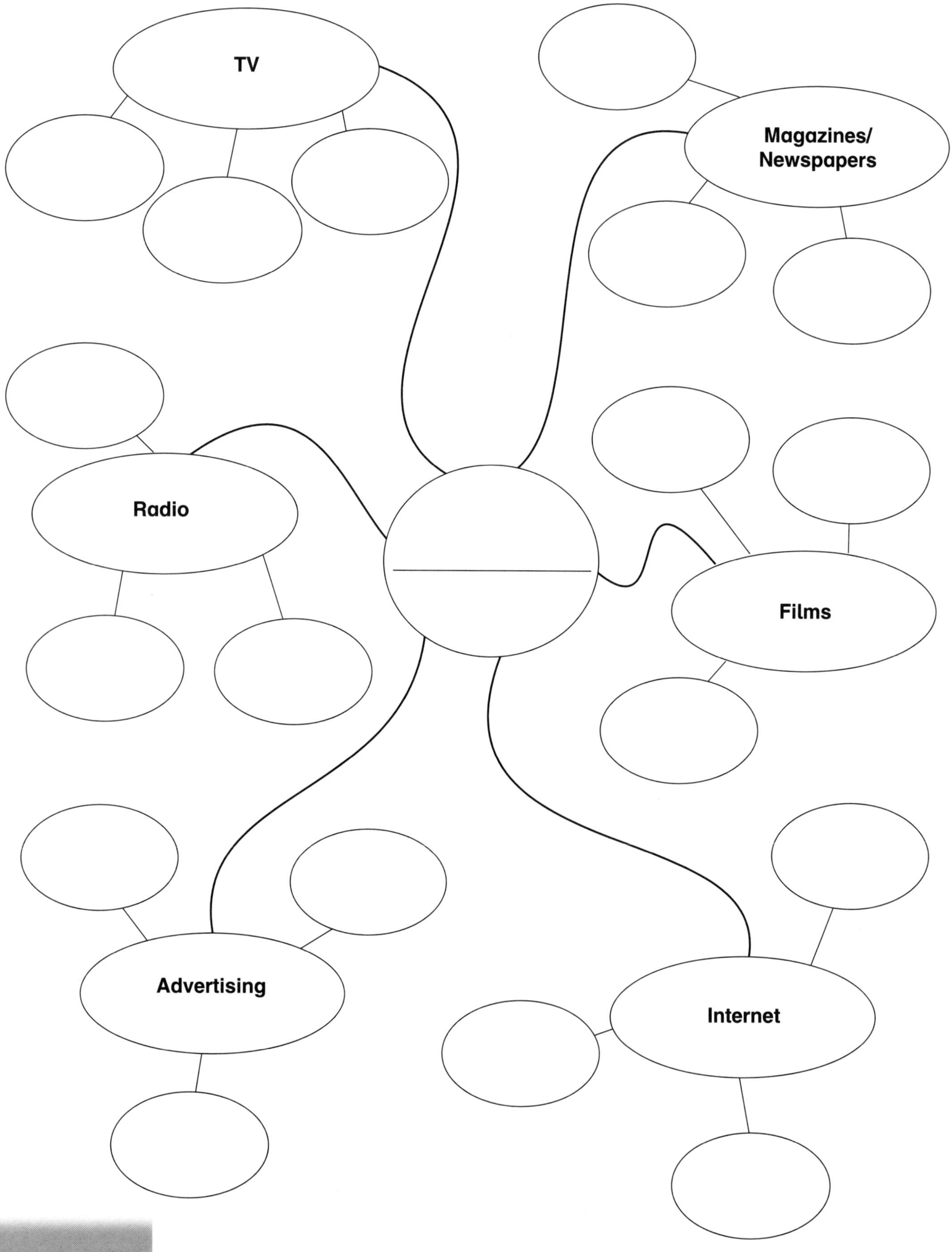

Worksheet
15.2

Student Book
Unit 15 • page 143

Audience for *Disney's Big Time*

Why does *Disney's Big Time* appeal to its audience? Write your reasons in the chart below.

Feature from the magazine cover	Reason why audience would like it
Title colours, style, and images	Look fun. More likely to appeal to boys.
Jimmy Neutron	Jimmy looks cool.
T.J. from *Recess*	
S Club 7	
Monsters from *Monsters, Inc.*	
Competition to win XBOX	
Competition to win trip to Disneyland	

Worksheet
15.3 *Kool* magazine

Student Book
Unit 15
◆ pages 144–145

Homework
15.1

Student Book
Unit 15 • page 143

Looking at a magazine cover

Name

What you have to do

1. **Find a magazine cover. It can come from home, from the library or from your teacher.**
2. **Complete the table about the audience for the magazine.**

What is the title of the magazine?	
Describe the main image on the cover.	
What are the main colours used on the cover?	
Is the style of the writing fun, or is it serious?	
What competitions are there?	
Write down what some of the articles are about.	
Is the magazine aimed at male or female readers? How do you know?	
How old do you think the readers might be?	
Who does the magazine belong to?	

Understanding the audience – how did I do?

Name	

Think about the work you have done about the audiences of magazine covers.

Tick the boxes to show what you are able to do.

In this unit:	I found this easy	I could do this with some help	I found this very difficult. I need to get better at this
1 I learned what 'audience' means when talking about the media.			
2 I learned to organise ideas in a mind map.			
3 I learned how to tell what the audience is for *Mizz* and *Disney's Big Time*.			
4 I used what I learned about audience to design part of the *Kool* cover.			
5 I gave a talk from notes to the publisher of *Kool*.			

I was best at ______________________________

I need to improve ______________________________

I will do this by ______________________________

Signed ______________________________

____

16 Persuading your audience

Student Book pages 148–155

Support for this unit
- Worksheets 16.1–16.3
- OHT 16.1
- Homework sheet 16.1
- Self-assessment sheet
- CD-ROM activity

Teaching and learning focus
- Writing a vivid description
- Understanding how writers and presenters persuade people

Objectives covered

Sentence level
- 2 Noun phrases
- 13e Persuasion

Text level – Reading
- 11 Print, sound and image
- 13 Non-fiction style

Text level – Writing
- 14 Evocative description

Speaking and Listening
- 8 Presentational techniques

16.1 Writing an effective description

Objectives S2, Wr14

1

Making links

1 Students sort a list of words into two groups – nouns and adjectives – exploring the function of vocabulary they will be using later.

2 The adjectives can be further sorted into 'unpleasant' (*dark*, *drab*, *damp*, *cold*, *dull*, *dirty*) and 'pleasant' (*warm*, *fresh*, *bright*, *cheerful*).

2

Whole class

Model text: Description of the writer's arrival at a dismal holiday cabin

- Discuss how each fact in the text can be checked.
- Explore why the adjectives make it seem awful. How do they make the reader feel and why?
- ***Extension*** Discuss the noun phrase, 'the colour of cold mushroom soup'. Use this example to model noun phrases that students might use in their own writing, i.e. *the colour of …*

1 Look at each of the three highlighted noun phrases and ask students to say what is the fact and what gives it its feeling.

Phrase	Fact	Feeling
Tired white walls	white walls	tired
Drab pink curtains	pink curtains	drab
Smell of damp socks	smell	damp socks

2 Recap how the writer has chosen words that will persuade the reader that this was an awful place.

3

Supported practice

Worksheet 16.1 supports this task

- Students work in pairs to rewrite the description. They should discuss which facts to keep and which to discard *before* starting writing.

4 **Independent work**

Worksheet 16.2 supports this task

- Students write a description of somewhere they have stayed. They include facts and feelings. The teacher can model this process and demonstrate how to build extended noun phrases.

5 **Securing the skills**

- Working as a class, students listen to each other's descriptions.

1 Can they identify the feeling of the place and how the writer has built up that feeling?

2 Can they suggest ways of making the description more persuasive? Encourage the use of noun phrases.

3 Encourage the class to respond to the description by giving reasons why they would not like to stay there.

> **Noun phrase:**
> - a single word, e.g. *wall,*
>   or when extended:
> - a group of words based on a noun as the head word, e.g. *creamy white walls, the colour of ice-cream*

16.2 Persuading listeners

N.B. There is no independent work in this section.

Objectives S13e, S&L8

1 **Making links**

- Students decide whether sentences are facts or opinions: *Facts: 1, 3, 5; Opinions 2, 4.*

2 **Whole class**

Model text: Example of a presenter persuading listeners to visit a holiday resort

OHT 16.1 supports this activity

- The features focused on are the use of: humour, exaggeration, description. The teacher needs to emphasise these features as the text is read out.

1 The facts readers learn about Falton are that it has: *donkeys; sandy beaches; sea you can swim in. It is a ten-minute drive from the town of San Antonio. At San Antonio there is lots of night life.*

2 Students list and exemplify the techniques to recap what they have learned:

The presenter makes you want to go there by using a) only positive opinions, such as '*it's such a friendly place*', '*fantastic sunsets*', etc; b) humour, such as '*even the donkeys are smiling*'; c) exaggeration, such as '*fantastic sunsets*', '*wonderful swimming*'. '*It's heaven*'; d) descriptions that make it sound fun, such as '*San Antonio really buzzes …*'

3 **Supported practice**

- Students read three quotations and identify the techniques presenters used to persuade the audience. Answers: *1 exaggeration; 2 humour; 3 touched listeners' feelings.*

4 **Securing the skills**

1 Students recall and list the techniques they have learned about.

2 They suggest an example of each technique to describe the cartoon of a barge holiday. For example, students might exaggerate the beauty of the scene in the foreground and make a joke about the factory in the background.

Consolidation Show a clip from a holiday travel programme and ask students to identify techniques used by the presenter to persuade viewers that a place is worth visiting.

16.3 Persuading readers

Objectives S13e, R11, R13

Homework sheet 16.1 supports this section

1 **Making links**

- Students recall the different persuasive techniques they have learned about. Brainstorm techniques that can be used to persuade listeners and readers to visit a place. Ask for examples of the techniques they suggest. You could introduce the topic of people being persuaded to choose holidays through advertisements, brochures, TV and radio programmes, etc.

2 **Whole class**

Model text: Advertisement from Club 18–30 holiday brochure

1 Identify why the text appeals to the 18–30 audience by finding: Two facts 18–30-year-olds will like: *there's a pool, free sun beds, bar with TV serving food, two beaches, town with bars and eateries.* One opinion they will like: *serious sunbathing sessions; scrummy food; enough bars and eateries for a massive night out.* Exaggeration about something important: *massive night out; The hotel is so well situated you'll have everything at your fingertips.* A description that builds a feeling that will appeal to them: *scrummy food; sizzling beaches; massive night out.*

2 Six things to look for: *headings, pictures, colour, print size, print style, use of space.*

3 **Supported practice**

Worksheet 16.3 supports this work

- These questions help students examine persuasive features used in a family holiday ad.

1 *Families.*

2 a) *The photograph of the happy family in the water together is given most space – it suggests readers can have fun spending time being together as a family.* b) *The brightest colours are used on the name of the resort, Golden Sands, and for the slogan: For a Fun Packed Family Holiday.* c) *The largest print is used for the headings; large coloured print is used for the headings that introduce different sections of information, such as, It's all on Park! Fantastic nights out... and a great family club room; Out and About... Explore the Area. The headings highlight features of the holiday that will persuade adults to choose it.*

3 Students search for: a) Exaggeration: *superb park, something for everyone, ... so much to do ...* b) Five facts: *can make sandcastles, go windsurfing, play golf ... Every night the entertainment is different ... plus most of the items in the lists.* c) One opinion: *fun-packed; superb park; lively atmosphere ...; Fantastic nights out; great family club room.*

4 Students explain to another pair how the persuasive techniques work.

4 **Independent work**

Worksheet 16.3 can be used to support this activity

This task provides an opportunity for assessment supported by the self-assessment sheet

1 The audience is people aged over 50.

2 Features that will appeal to this audience: *photographs of people in this age group enjoying the holiday; large print saying 'over 50s'; bold print saying 'Fun packed, full entertainment'; the choice of activities – Frank Sinatra, sing-alongs, bingo, bowls, afternoon's dancing with tea and scones, etc.; opinions, e.g. Queen Victoria pub is a great place to relax, unwind and meet new friends.*

3 These things will work because the audience: *can see people like them enjoying the holiday; know only people in their age group will go; will be doing activities they enjoy.*

5 **Securing the skills**

- Ask the class to suggest ideas for an advertisement to appeal to people of their own age and persuade them to spend a weekend at a theme park. Students should use the suggested techniques and mention: wonderful rides, great accommodation, lots of young people, places to eat, etc.

  Extension: Students could make up their own holiday advertisement modelled on the ones they have read. It could be based on a holiday place they have been to, or describe the area where they live as a place to visit on holiday.

Worksheet
16.1

Describing a cheerful holiday cabin

Student Book
Unit 16 • page 149

Rewrite the description of the cabin on page 149. Make it seem a cheerful place. Keep some of the facts. Change some of the adjectives.

1 Which facts do you want to change?

Old fact	New fact
It was drizzling	*The sun was shining*

2 Write your new description. Use adjectives from the box below.
Add some of your own.

warm	fresh	cheerful	bright	cosy	fragrant (*smells lovely*)

When we arrived at the cabin ____________________ . Each cabin was ________________ . Ours also had _______________ .

We pushed open the door and ________________________ .

The five of us ____________________ . We looked around at the __________________ and ____________________ .

There was a ______________________________ .

This was ______________________ !

Describing a place

Student Book
nit 16 • page 149

Describe a place where you have stayed. Put in facts and feelings. Tell your reader what it was really like.

1 Where did you stay? ____________

2 Write down *five* **facts** about the place.

a I could see ____________

b The ____________ were ____________

c ____________ smelt ____________

d ____________

e ____________

3 What did the place feel like? Circle one word that describes how it felt, or write one of your own.

cheerful miserable creepy ____________

4 Read the words in the box. Underline *five* adjectives (describing words) you can use to build that feeling. Then add *three* more of your own.

warm	old	drab	ghostly	fresh	cold
strange	dirty	cheerful	dark	bright	damp
cosy	dull	gloomy	________	________	________

5 Now use your facts and describing words. Write your description.

I stayed at ____________. The first thing I saw

was ____________. It had ____________.

There was ____________.

I looked around at ____________.

The ____________ was ____________

and ____________. This was ____________!

Persuading readers

Student Book
Unit 16 • page 154

Read the advertisement about Golden Sands holiday park. Then answer the questions below.

1 What audience does the advert appeal to?

It appeals to ________________ . I know this because ____________________

____

2 a What is given a lot of space? Why?

Most space is given to ____

This is so that ____

____

b What is in bright colours? Why?

__________________________________ is in bright colours. They make you

notice ____

The writer wants you to notice ______________________________ because

____

____

c What is in large print or in bold? Why?

The words in large print are ____

These are important because ____

____

The words in different colours are _____________________________________

These are important because ____

____

OHT

16.1 Persuading listeners

Student Book
it 16 • page 150

2 **Television and radio presenters want listeners to remember their opinions. Read this example. Then answer the questions below.**

> Falton is such a friendly place even the donkeys are smiling. The beaches are so beautiful ... it's amazing here. Fantastic sunsets, gorgeous sand and wonderful swimming. It's heaven ... and it's only a ten-minute drive from town. After a hard day's sunbathing it is time to take in the night life. And San Antonio really buzzes at night. It's non-stop party time.

1 What facts did you learn about Falton?

2 How does the presenter try to make you want to go there?

Homework
16.1

Student Book
Unit 16 • page 152

Persuading readers

Name	

What you have to do

1. **Find a large advert which has a colour picture.**
2. **Read it carefully. Answer the questions. Then fill in the chart below.**
3. ***Afterwards*, stick your advert to the back of this piece of paper.**

1 **Who** is the advert trying to persuade? ______________________

2 **What** does it want those readers to do? ______________________

	What is it?	**Why will it persuade readers?**
1 What takes up the most space?		
2 What is in the brightest colours?		
3 What is in large print?		
4 What is in **bold** print?		
5 What is in *italics*?		
6 Find a fact.		
7 Find an opinion.		
8 Find any exaggeration.		

Persuading an audience – how did I do?

Name	

Think about the work you have done on persuading your audience. Tick the boxes to show what you can do.

In this unit:	I found this easy	I could do this with some help	I found this very difficult. I need to get better at this
1 I worked out who an advert appealed to.			
2 I found what took up **most space.**			
3 I found what was in **large or coloured print**.			
4 I found **facts**.			
5 I found **opinions**.			
6 I found **exaggeration**.			
7 I explained why each feature would persuade readers to go on this holiday.			

I was best at ______________________

I need to improve ______________________

I will do this by______________________

Signed ______________________

____

17 Putting your point of view

Student Book pages 156–167

Support for this unit
- Worksheets 17.1–17.4
- OHT sheet 17.1
- Homework sheet 17.1
- Self-assessment sheet
- CD-ROM activities

Teaching and learning focus
- Backing up an opinion in a talk
- Finding out how a writer supports the main ideas in a text
- Persuading readers an opinion is right

Objectives covered

Sentence level
- 1 Subordinate clauses
- 3 Boundary punctuation
- 10 Paragraph structure
- 11 Sentence variety
- 13e Persuasion

Text level – Reading
- 7 Identify main ideas

Text level – Writing
- 15 Express a view
- 16 Validate an argument

Speaking and Listening
- 5 Put a point of view

17.1

Backing up your point of view

Objective S&L5

1

Making links
- Students extend their vocabulary by deciding which phrase in each sentence shows it is an opinion.

2

Whole class

Model text: Annotated opinion about a class trip
- Use the text of a speech to demonstrate how a talk that gives an opinion and backs it up should be organised. Model answer: *C, A, B, D.*

3

Supported practice

Worksheet 17.1 supports this activity
- Students work in pairs to prepare a talk arguing for where to go on a trip. Some pairs may need support in choosing a trip. You may need to model using the chart.

4

Independent work
- Students work with other pairs, giving their talk and deciding whose opinion is backed up most strongly, and why. Make sure they are not simply judging which trip they would prefer.

5

Securing the skills

1 Students give their talks in front of the rest of the class and pick out which points are well supported. When they discuss how to make opinions stronger, provide examples.

2 The students can then vote on where they would like to go. Make sure that they vote on the basis of what they have heard, not on their previous experience or opinion.

- ***Extension*** Let students take part in a more formal debate with a smaller panel of speakers. Let listeners ask questions about different places before voting.

17.2

How writers organise and support their points

Objectives S10, R7

1

Making links
- Students identify what job(s) each sentence is doing. Help them to understand that sentences often do more than one job. A *a;* B *b, c;* C *d, e;* D *a, d;* E *a, f.*

2 **Whole class**

Model text: Student's opinion on class trip

OHT 17.1 supports this work

- Students may need to be reminded what exaggeration (dealt with in Unit 16) is before attempting this work. Use the first paragraph of the text to demonstrate how writers organise their written opinions, and what job each sentence is doing to contribute to the opinion.

1 Students work with you to see how the second paragraph is organised and what job each sentence is doing.

3 **Supported practice**

Worksheet 17.2 supports this activity

- Students work in pairs and decide what jobs different sentences do. This helps them to understand how the writer has backed up his argument.
- Using Worksheet 17.2 makes it easier to differentiate the task by: giving different pairs of students different sentences; giving a different number of sentences to label to different pairs; letting students work as individuals or in pairs – they are given a sentence and the right labels which they have to stick on to the right part of the sentence. You may prefer to photocopy Worksheet 17.2 to A3 size.

4 **Independent work**

Homework sheet 17.1 reinforces this activity

- Students follow a plan and write two paragraphs about how the writer argued that The Bounce is the best ride at Oakwood. This is an opportunity for level 3 students to practise writing about a text. It is useful to remind them how to use quotation marks.

5 **Securing the skills**

- Discuss with the students whether the writer has succeeded in persuading them that The Bounce is the best ride. As you draw out their reasons, make sure that they refer back to the textual features of the paragraph.

17.3 Writing longer persuasive sentences

Objectives S1, S3

1 **Making links**

- Help students identify which sentences make one or two points, and which have most impact and/or give most information.

2 **Whole class**

Model text: Building up a longer sentence

- Use the steps in the book to demonstrate how to write a complex sentence that gives both a fact and an opinion. Show that there are different ways of writing the same sentence.

1–3 Help students to decide which form of sentence is the most persuasive: *Go Zone, which is open from May to September, is the best theme park.*

4 Support the students as they write a complex sentence with a fact and an opinion in it.

Extension: Explain about the two types of clauses used to build a complex sentence: **main clauses** that make sense on their own, and **subordinate clauses** that depend on the main clause to make sense.

3 **Supported practice**

Worksheet 17.3 provides differentiation for this activity

- Students work in pairs to write four complex sentences using the facts and opinions in the list. Make sure that students do not use 'and' to join the sentences.

4 **Independent work**

- Students use the complex sentences they constructed in a paragraph persuading people to visit Go Zone.

5 **Securing the skills**

- Students work together to redraft a paragraph so that it contains some persuasive sentences. Ensure that they use the techniques they have learned in this section to build some complex sentences containing 'which'.

  Extension: Teachers can show how other connectives such as *because, so, since, although, if*, etc., can be used to build longer sentences. N.B. Avoid the term 'complex sentence' as they will be producing compound sentences as well.

17.4 Putting your point of view

Objectives S11, S13e, Wr15, Wr16

1 **Making links**

- Students work as a class while you act as scribe.

1 Students suggest examples of sentences that do different jobs.

2 They then check whether any of their examples are sentences doing more than one job. Be prepared to provide some examples that do: *Nemesis is hair-raising, isn't it? I'd like to go on it a million times!*

2 **Whole class**

- Two standard rhetorical question structures are given as models to help students suggest their own rhetorical questions. This is an opportunity to encourage inventive thinking.

3 **Supported practice**

Model text: Steps to write a point of view

Worksheet 17.4 supports this activity

- Work with the class to follow a series of steps showing how to write a text arguing for the theme park ride of their choice. The teacher needs to model each step but students should end up with their own sentences to argue for their own choice of ride.

4 **Independent work**

- Students collate their work and write a best copy of their argument. As this is an opportunity for students to practise their drafting skills, elicit from the class how to go about this before they begin.

5 **Securing the skills**

- Students work as a class. They listen to each other's arguments and identify what makes an argument persuasive, trying to bring out one good point in each piece.

Worksheet
17.1 Backing up your point of view

Student Book
Unit 17 • page 158

1 **Work in pairs. Where have you been that would make a good class outing? Persuade the rest of the class and your teacher that this is the best place to go on a trip. Note your ideas in the frame below.**

2 **Now practise explaining your opinion. Take it in turns to make points.**

Opinion

1 Where should your class go?

____________ to go would be ____________

Three reasons (points) why this is the best trip to go on	Connectives you could use: *therefore, so, because, since*	Reasons backed up by
1 *It is* ________	________	a fact: ________
2 *You can* ________	________	an example from your own experience: ________
3 *There is/are* ________	________	what it could be like: ________

Worksheet

17.2

Student Book
Unit 17 • page 162

Supporting your point of view

1 Cut out the labels and the sentences.

2 Stick the right labels on each of the sentences below. Remember, each sentence can have more than one label.

Fact	Fact	Fact	Fact	Fact
What The Bounce is like	What The Bounce is like			
An exclamation	An exclamation	An exclamation		
Exaggeration	Exaggeration	Question		
Opinion	Opinion	Opinion	Opinion	

1 By far the best ride at Oakwood is The Bounce.

2 You have to pay extra to go on it (it was £30 when I went), but it's really worth it!

3 It will take up to three people at a time, so each group can split the cost between them.

4 That's really good, isn't it?

5 The Bounce is very popular because it is just like doing a bungee jump.

6 You are lifted up very high and strapped into a special safety harness.

7 Then one of you pulls a handle and you just DROP!

8 The rope goes really tight and you swing for ages so it is really frightening!

9 It's the most frightening thing in the world.

Student Book
Unit 17
• pages 164–165

Writing longer sentences

Work in pairs. Make four longer sentences.

1 Read the facts and opinions below.

2 Write the number of the opinion that matches each fact, below.

Fact	Opinion
A	2
B	______
C	______
D	______

1 Use a fact and opinion in each sentence. Cut out one pair at a time.

2 Glue the two parts of the sentence together to make a longer sentence.

3 Stick your four longer sentences onto a piece of paper.

Facts

A	Go Zone has over 50 different attractions and rides
B	It has 100 acres of gardens
C	The children enjoy going on the Adventure Playground
D	There are eight places to eat

Opinions

1	which are very beautiful.
2	which are great fun.
3	which are great value.
4	which is very safe.

Worksheet
17.4

Student Book
Unit 17
◆ pages 166–167

Writing your point of view

Step 1 Decide which is the best theme park ride that you have been on.

Write down your opinion.

___

___

Step 2 Work out different ways to back up your point of view.

Fill in the chart below. Write three sentences of each type.

Facts	Examples	Opinions
1	1	1
2	2	2
3	3	3

Step 3 Work out how to make your writing persuasive.

Write four different sentences about your ride.

a A sentence that exaggerates
b A complex sentence that has a fact and an opinion in it
c A sentence that asks a question that people will agree with
d A short sentence that is an exclamation

OHT
17.1

Student Book
Unit 17
pages 160–161

How writers organise and support their points

Oakwood Park

I think the best theme park for our class to go to is Oakwood Park. Some of the other theme parks I've been to were so busy you had to queue for over an hour to go on a ride. If you have to spend a lot of time in queues, then you can't go on so many rides, can you? Then, when you do finally get on the ride, it's all over so quickly. That is a total let-down!

[1] In my opinion Oakwood Park is very good value. [2] It is much cheaper than a lot of the other theme parks, probably because it is smaller. [3] It would not be too expensive, so everyone could come on the trip. [4] That's got to be good, hasn't it? [5] We could even get round all the rides in one day as it is smaller! It's the best theme park in the world!

Homework
17.1

Student Book
Unit 17 • page 162

What jobs is each sentence doing?

Name	

What you have to do

Read each sentence. Tick each job you think it is doing.

Remember: each sentence may do more than one job.

Sentence	Fact	Opinion	Question	Exaggeration	Exclamation
1 Chocolate milk shakes are the best, and they are really good for you too!					
2 Chocolate contains huge amounts of iron, which your body needs.					
3 I could eat a chocolate ice-cream as big as a horse!					
4 Do you like white chocolate or plain chocolate best?					
5 Who can stop eating delicious creamy milk chocolate?					

Putting a point of view – how did I do?

Name	

Think about the work you have done in this unit. Tick the boxes to show what you are able to do.

In this unit:	I found this easy	I could do this with some help	I found this very difficult. I need to get better at this
1 I told the difference between a fact and an opinion.			
2 I argued for my point of view and gave different sorts of reasons.			
3 I worked out how someone had put together the argument they had written.			
4 I wrote complex sentences.			
5 I wrote an argument.			
6 I used different sorts of sentences in my argument.			

I was best at ____________________

I need to improve ____________________

I will do this by ____________________

Signed ____________________

____

18 Presenting a balanced argument

Student Book pages 168–175

Support for this unit
- Worksheets 18.1–18.2
- OHT sheet 18.1
- Homework sheet 18.1
- Self-assessment sheet
- CD-ROM activities

Teaching and learning focus
- Saying and writing what you think
- Listening to and writing about what other people think

Objectives covered

Word level
- 18 Qualification and comparison
- 20 Connectives

Sentence level
- 10 Paragraph structure
- 12 Sequencing paragraphs
- 13f Discursive writing

Text level – Reading
- 9 Distinguish writer's views

Text level – Writing
- 10 Organise texts appropriately
- 16 Validate an argument
- 18 Present findings

Speaking and Listening
- 14 Modify views

18.1 Different points of view

Objectives R9, S&L14

1 **Making links**
- Establish that 'I think' makes this a point of view. Ask students if they know another word for point of view (*opinion*). Ask several students to give a point of view about school uniform using 'I think ...'. Encourage them to give a reason as well.

2 **Whole class**

Model text: Mock newspaper article on wearing school uniform
- Establish that the extract is from an article and read the text aloud. Look together at the annotations. Ask students to speculate about where they might see an article like this, then ask them the questions.

3 **Supported practice**

1 Explain that students must listen to each other's points of view very carefully. They may change their mind about something when they hear what their partner says.

2 When pairs have finished, take feedback and ask if anyone has changed their mind because of what they have heard, or has heard a persuasive argument.

4 **Independent practice**

Worksheet 18.1 offers some extension of phrases to show points of view

1 Model the talk using the head teacher's talk. Highlight the phrases, *'In my opinion, ...', 'I know ... but ...'* and *'I think ...'*.

2 Ask students to gather their thoughts for a minute before talking to their partner.

5 **Securing the skills**

1 If this activity can be recorded on video, it will be very powerful for students. After the talks, feed back to the class the strengths of their performances.

2 Discuss whether anyone has changed their minds, and why.

18.2 Finding out what people think

Objectives W18, Wr16

Homework sheet 18.1 reinforces these activities

1 **Making links**

- Students need to understand what a survey is and how it can be used to gather people's views. Ask if they have done surveys in other curriculum areas or in KS2.

2 **Whole class**

Model text: Survey results on school uniform

OHT 18.1 supports this activity

1 Look at the survey and read through the questions in it. Then go through question 1 to make sure that students can understand the results.

2 Write 'most' and 'a few' on the board or flipchart. Establish whether the sentence is true or false.

- Ask the question, 'Who likes school uniform in class 7A?' Then ask a student to say a correct sentence using 'most' or 'a few'. You could ask several questions like this to make sure students are confident with 'most' and 'a few'.

3 **Supported practice**

- Explain the task to the students, checking that they are clear about using the information in the chart.

4 **Independent practice**

Worksheet 18.2 contains the blank survey grid to support this activity

- Ensure that students know to ask everyone in the class and how to represent each response with a tick. After the survey, perhaps show students how to total up the survey.

5 **Securing the skills**

- Students could prepare a sentence using 'most' or 'a few' to describe the findings of their surveys before the whole class feedback.
- After the feedback, a possible extra homework could be to write up the findings of their survey in sentences using 'most' and 'a few'.

18.3 Writing what you think

Objectives W20, S10, S13f, Wr18

Note: This section does not follow the usual pattern. The section is organised to support the students in extended writing by teaching each part of the essay separately.

1 **Making links**

- Rehearse the true sentences orally before asking students to write them down. Ask students to read out their sentences and see if the class are all in agreement.

2 **Whole class**

Model text: Mock up of student's opinion

- Read the paragraph to the students and check that they have understood.
- Ask what a topic sentence is. If they don't know, explain that it's the main sentence in a paragraph which tells you what the whole paragraph is about. The rest of the paragraph gives you more information about the topic sentence.
- Go through the questions with the class.

3 **Supported practice**

- Ask students to find their surveys. Orally rehearse the paragraph using the writing frame. You might ask the class to think of all the reasons why you might or might not like uniform to help those who are not yet sure what they think.
- Students write the paragraph. Ask them to check their work with a partner.
- As an alternative, you could demonstrate the writing using this paragraph.

4 **Independent practice**

- Students should be able to manage this fairly independently. Monitor what students are writing to check that they understand what they are doing. At the end of the paragraph, ask students to check their partner's work.
- Feed back to the class any errors that you have seen while monitoring the class.

5 **Securing the skills**

- Point out the topic sentences and explain how to use them to write the next two paragraphs. Take feedback and highlight successful examples of writing.

18.4

Presenting an argument

Objectives S12, Wr10, Wr18

Note: As in the previous section, students are taught to write each part of the essay separately, to give maximum support.

1 **Making links**

- Students often find acknowledging the points of view of others quite difficult. Emphasise the need to listen to others and possibly modify or confirm their own views.

2 **Whole class**

Model text: Mock newspaper article on school uniform

- Read through the text and ask students which parts they have seen before.
- Take students through the questions and annotations. Draw attention to the verb forms 'to introduce' and 'to conclude' to help students understand the functions of the introductory and concluding paragraphs.
- You may ask students to note down the definitions of introduction and conclusion for later reference.

3 **Supported practice**

- Students could read aloud to a partner the four paragraphs they have written.
- Orally rehearse the introduction to help students write the introduction. Ask students to check their paragraph with their partner. Hear several examples.

4 **Independent practice**

- Refer back to the conclusion of the model text to remind students, and perhaps model the conclusion orally. After checking in pairs, hear a few conclusions.

5 **Securing the skills**

1, 2 Explain the task to students and emphasise the need for good presentation.

3 When students have finished, hear several examples to celebrate their good work.

Worksheet

18.1 Points of view

Student Book
nit 18 • page 169

1 Write three phrases for giving opinions.

1 ______________________________

2 ______________________________

3 ______________________________

2 Read this text. The speaker is the cook in a school. Find the five phrases that tell you that this is someone's point of view.

No more chips!

'What do I think about school dinners? Well, if you ask me, students get a good deal. Personally speaking, I think that there is a good choice on the menu. But all they want is chips! Chips with everything! I know students like chips, but they should eat other things too. In my opinion, they should have no choice! I would give them meat and two veg every day – no chips!'

1 ______________________________

2 ______________________________

3 ______________________________

4 ______________________________

5 ______________________________

3 Can you add any more phrases for giving opinions to the list?

1 ______________________________

2 ______________________________

3 ______________________________

Worksheet

18.2 School uniform survey

Student Book
Unit 18 • page 171

1 **Ask *all* the other students in your class to answer the questions in the survey.**

2 **Put a tick in the correct 'yes' or 'no' box for every answer.**

3 **Add up the ticks in each box at the end of the survey.**

Questions	Yes	No
Do you like school uniform?	Total =	Total =
Do you prefer trainers to shoes?	Total =	Total =
Would school be like a fashion show if students chose what to wear?	Total =	Total =
Would students get bullied if they chose what to wear?	Total =	Total =

OHT
18.1

Finding out what people think

Student Book
nit 18 • page 170

School uniform survey		
Questions	**Yes**	**No**
Do you like school uniform?	2	8
Do you prefer trainers to shoes?	8	2
Would school be like a fashion show if students chose what to wear?	3	7
Would students get bullied if they chose what to wear?	6	4

Most students don't like school uniform.

A few students like school uniform.

Homework

18.1 School dinner survey

Student Book
Unit 18
• pages 170–171

Name

What you have to do

1 **Read the survey below about what students think about school dinners in Dawson Comprehensive.**

2 **Write about the results and give your own opinion, below.**

Questions	Yes	No
Do you like chips?	16	4
Do you prefer chips to baked potatoes?	13	7
Would you like there to be only one choice for school dinners?	2	18
Would you like to have chips only once a week?	4	16

1 Write *four* sentences about the results of the survey using 'most' or 'a few'.

1 ______________________________

2 ______________________________

3 ______________________________

4 ______________________________

2 Write *two* sentences giving your point of view about school dinners.

1 ______________________________

____

____

2 ______________________________

____

____

Presenting a balanced argument – how did I do?

Name	

Think about the work you have done on presenting a balanced argument.

Tick the boxes to show what you are able to do.

In this unit:	I found this easy	I could do this with some help	I found this very difficult I need to get better at this.
1 I spoke about my point of view on school uniform.			
2 I found out what other people think using a survey.			
3 I used 'most' and 'a few' to talk about the results of a survey.			
4 I wrote six paragraphs about different points of view on school uniform.			
5 I looked at what an introduction and a conclusion do in a piece of writing.			

I was best at ____________________

I need to improve ____________________

I will do this by ____________________

Signed ____________________

Which strategy card do I want?

- **Find the card that will help you on the list below:**

Skim the text to find out what it is about →	Card 2
Scan the text to find information →	Card 3
Read closely to understand details →	Card 4
Make sense of what I am reading →	Card 5
There is a word I don't know →	Card 6
Making notes →	Card 7
Plan: How should I write about this? →	Card 8
Write in sentences: Think it, say it, write it →	Card 9
After writing: improving my work →	Card 10
Checking my punctuation →	Card 11
Working in a group →	Card 12
I want to remember something →	Card 13

Skim the text to find out what it is about

Focus: Skimming

1 Search for features of layout.

Find and read each of these:

- Headings
- Subheadings
- Large print
- Bold print
- Italics

KEEP ASKING → What is it about?

2 Find and read each of these:

- Introduction – first paragraph
- First and last sentence of each paragraph
- Conclusion – last paragraph

PAUSE AND ASK → What does this tell me?

Strategy card

3

Focus: Scanning

Scan the text to find information

Step 1

ASK: What am I looking for? Search the question for clues:

Who – search for names (look for capital letters)
What – search for an explanation
When – search for times, dates, months, seasons
Why – search for reasons
Where – search for place names (look for capital letters)
How – search for the way things happen

Step 2

READ:

- Headings
- Large print
- Bold print
- Text in boxes
- Pictures and captions

Step 3

USE MY FINGER to search long pieces of writing:

- Sweep my finger across line by line
- Only stop when I see what I need
- Underline or make a note of it.

Read closely to understand details

Focus:
Reading for meaning

Step 1

BEFORE reading, ask:

- What do I need to find out?
- What am I going to do with the information?

Step 2

WHILE you are reading, ask:

- What does this tell me?
- How does this link with what I already know?
- What can I guess from this?

Step 3

KEEP PAUSING to ask:

- What have I found out so far?
- Can I picture this?
- Other questions, for example, *Who ...? What ...? Why ...?*

Strategy card

5

Focus:
Reading for meaning

Make sense of what I am reading

If you don't understand what you read, follow the steps below.

Step 1

Read it again:

slowly + out loud + pausing for punctuation

Ask: What is happening?

Step 2

Read around it:

- Read back a bit – search for names
- Read on a bit
- Now try reading it again

Step 3

Search for these clues:

- Punctuation

  Ask: what does it tell me? *This is a question; this is a speech ...*
- Link words, for example, *then, after, but, because ...*

  Ask: what do they tell me?

Step 4

Rewrite any long sentences:

- **Find** the part that makes sense on its own. **Write** it as a sentence.
- **Ask:** What is the rest of the sentence describing? **Write** this as a sentence.

Step 5

Check you understand it now:

- **Ask:**

  1 What have I found out?

  2 How does this fit in with what I already know?

ategy card
6

Focus:
Reading for
meaning

There is a word I don't know

FIRST Try one of these strategies, then check your idea out below.

Strategy 1 Re-reading
Read the whole sentence or paragraph again slowly. Then guess what this word must mean.

Strategy 2 Look for parts of the word you already know

Strategy 3 Ask: what job is the word doing in the sentence?

Strategy 4 Use a dictionary

THEN Check: Have I worked out the right meaning?

1 Say the sentence again using your own words.

2 **Ask:** does it make sense?

- If the answer is **NO:** Try some of the other strategies.

- If the answer is **YES:** Well done! Carry on reading!

Strategy card
7

Focus:
Writing notes

Making notes

Step 1

Ask:

- Why am I making notes?
- What do I want to find out? → What are the **key words** I am looking for? **List** those key words.
- What is the best way to organise my notes?

Listed as bullet points?

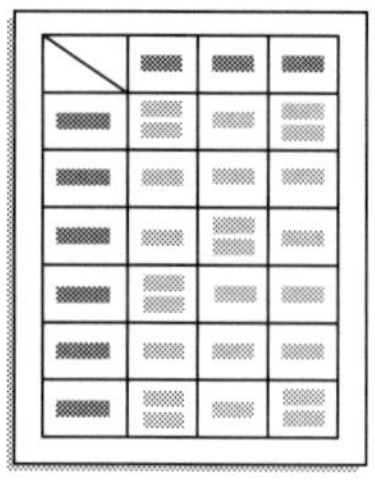

In a table or grid?

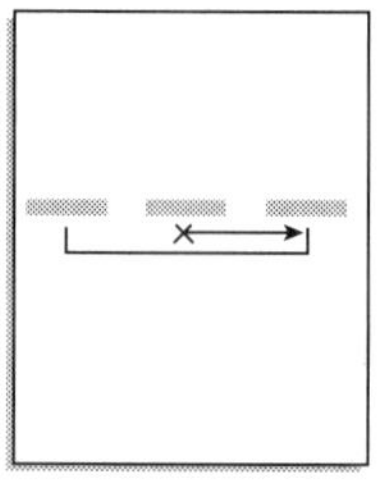

As a time line?

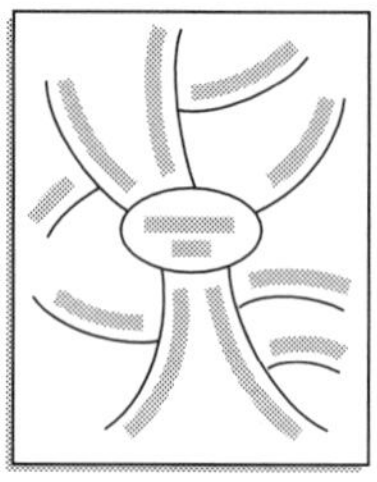

As a mind map?

Other?

Step 2

Skim and scan:

- Skim to find where the information is.
- Then scan for key words.

Step 3

Choose which part to note down by asking:

- Which part do I need?
- What can I leave out?

Step 4

Write:

- Don't write in full sentences.
- Use figures and short forms *(e.g., &, etc.)*.
- Give each point a number or a bullet.

ategy card
8

Focus:
lanning writing

Plan: How should I write about this?

Step 1

Ask:

- What am I writing about?
- Who am I writing for?
- What type of text am I writing? For example, is it: *a story*? ... *a report*? ... *an explanation*?
- What do I know about writing this type of text?

Step 2

Choose the best planning frame for the type of text:

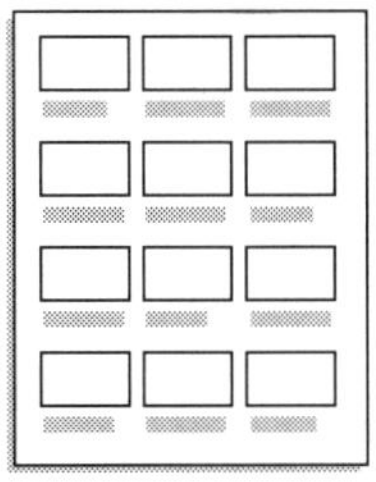
story board

list

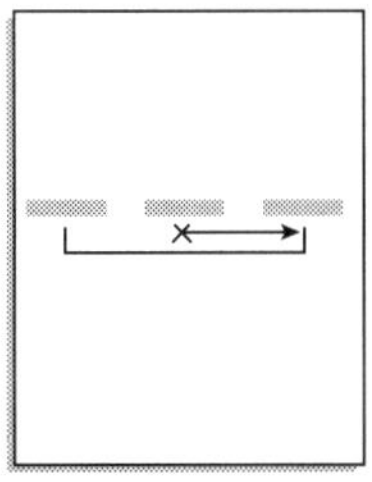
time line

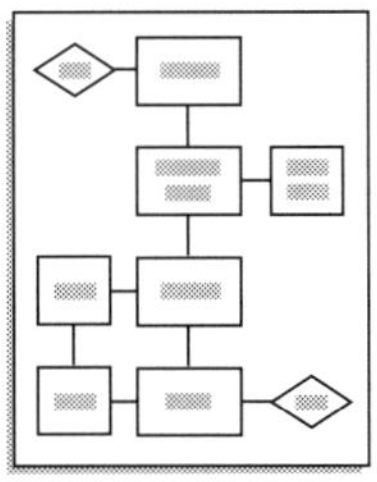
flow chart

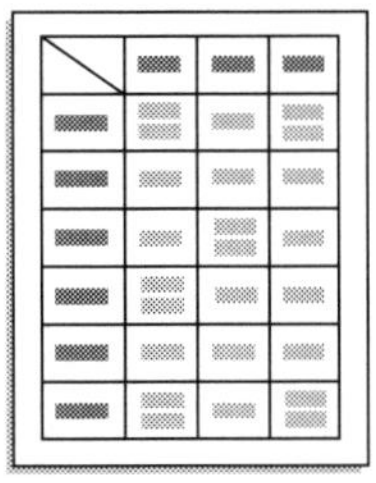
chart

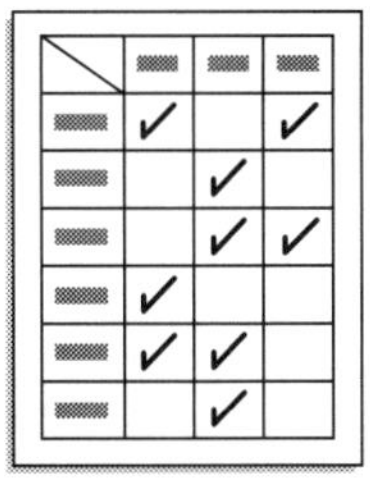
grid

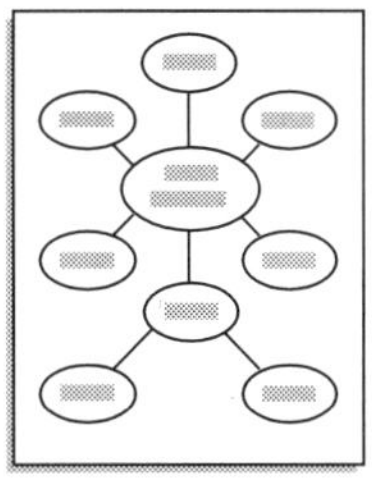
spider diagram

Step 3

Write a plan:

- Write your notes
- **Ask:** What is most important? Give points letters A, B, C, ...
- Number your points in the order you will write about them.

Step 4

Think about how texts like this are normally written. Ask:

- How should it look?
- How should it sound? *Informal? Formal?...*

Strategy card 9

Focus: Writing

Write in sentences: Think it, say it, write it

Follow these three steps as you write

Step 1 Think it

Ask:

- What does it need to say?
- How can I say this?

Step 2 Say it

- Practise saying it out loud in your head.

Ask:

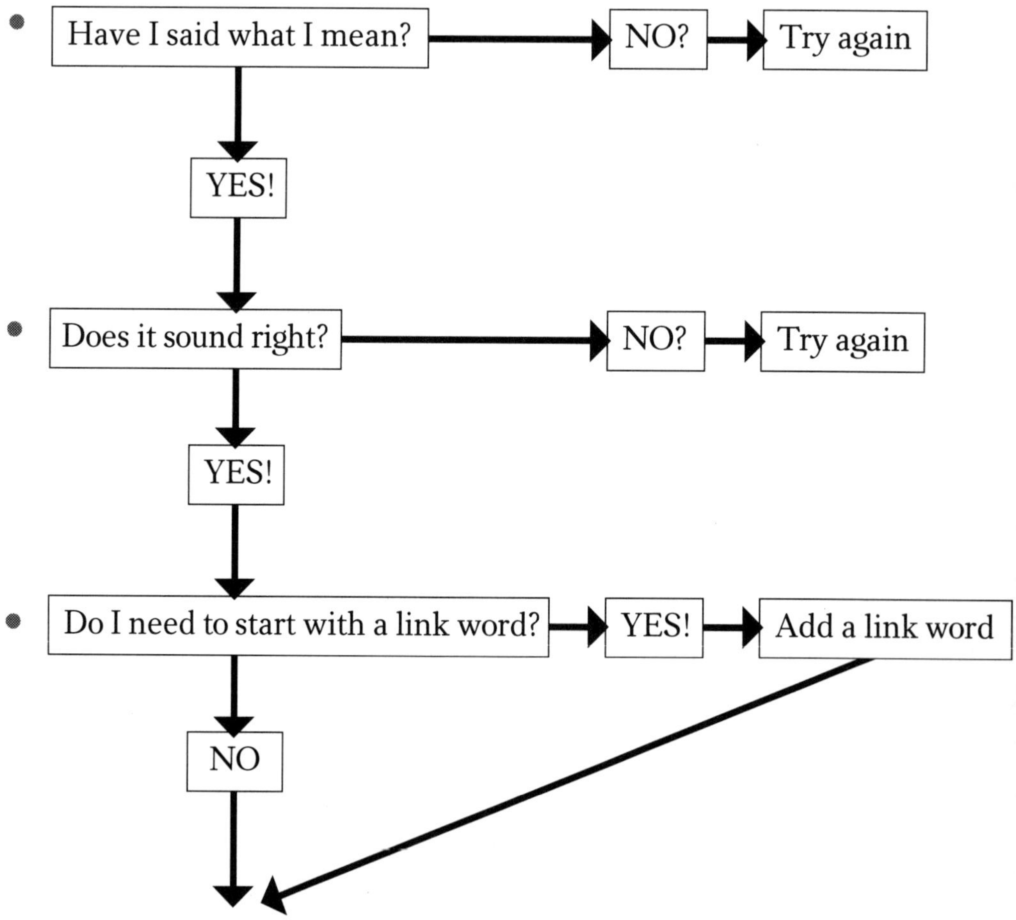

Step 3 Write it

- Say the sentence out loud in your head as you write it.
- Begin with a capital letter.
- Remember to use punctuation.

After writing: improving my work

Focus: Editing for structure, grammar and punctuation

When you have finished your writing:

- check that your message is clear
- improve the text as much as you can.

Step 1

Look at the way you set out the whole text.
Ask:

- Is there an introduction and a conclusion?
- Does each paragraph have a different main point?
- Are the points in a sensible order?
- Have I used link words?

Step 2

Check your sentences.

- **Read** each sentence. **Ask:** Does it make sense?
- **Investigate** sentences that don't make sense. **Ask:** Is it clear who is doing what?
- **Investigate** longer sentences. **Ask:** Does each part make sense?

Step 3

Check your choice of words.
Ask:

- Does each word mean what I want to say?
- Is there a better word?
- Does the word look right?
- Have I repeated any words?

Strategy card 11

Focus: Editing

Checking my punctuation

Step 1

Scan the text. Check your setting out.
Ask:

- Have I organised my writing into paragraphs?
- Is it clear where each new paragraph starts?

> - Have I used the right punctuation?
> - What do I need to change?

Step 2

Read the text slowly, and say it out loud in your head.
Ask:

- Have I shown readers when to pause so it makes sense?
- What job is this sentence doing? For example: *Asking a question; It's speech.*
- What punctuation does it need to show this? For example: *a question mark*

> - Have I used the right punctuation?
> - What do I need to change?

Step 3

Look at the words.
Ask:

- Is this a proper name? → Does it begin with a capital letter?
- Does it start a sentence? → Does it begin with a capital letter?
- Are there letters missing? → Have I used an apostrophe (')?
- Does this word show that a thing belongs to someone? → Have I used an apostrophe (')?

> - Have I used the right punctuation?
> - What do I need to change?

'ategy card
12

Focus:
Speaking and listening

Working in a group

Step 1

Before: Plan

Ask:

- What is the task?
- Who is doing each of these jobs:
  - Chairperson?
  - Taking notes?
  - Feeding back to the rest of the class?

Step 2

During: Take part

- Speak clearly and loudly enough.
- Take it in turns to speak. Don't interrupt!
- Bring others in by asking, 'What do you think?'
- Listen to what others say. Show you have by:
  - asking questions
  - commenting
  - making links.
- Keep to the point.

Step 3

After: How well did I do?

Ask:

- Did I join in?
- Did I let everyone else talk too?
- Did I listen to others?
- Did I help to make sure we finished the task?
- How can I improve?

Strategy card
13

Focus:
Thinking skills

I want to remember something

Follow these six steps to help you remember something.

Step 1 Really WANT TO remember it.

- Have a good reason for wanting to remember it, for example: *So that I can do well.*

Step 2 Make sure you understand the information you want to remember.

Step 3 Go over it in lots of different ways:

- Write it
- Say it
- Read it out loud
- Act it out
- Sing it
- Turn it into some colourful notes
- Picture it
- Tell someone else about it
- Walk around reading it

Step 4 Use a memory trick:

- Make a mnemonic using the first letters of the key words, for example: ***R**ichard of **Y**ork **G**ave **B**attle **I**n **V**ain – to remember the six colours of the rainbow (**r**ed, **y**ellow, **g**reen, **b**lue, **i**ndigo, **v**iolet)*
- Tell the information as a story.
- Link it to things you already know.
- Make a colourful cartoon of it in your mind.

Step 5 Tell it to someone else.

Step 6 Keep on recalling it:

- ten minutes later
- again in the evening
- again the next day.

Non-fiction text types

Text type	Structure	Language features
Recount Tells the reader about an event or events	• Opening usually gives background details, e.g. when, where, who • Series of events in chronological order	• Past tense • Active voice • Some use of connectives of time (e.g. *then*, *next*) and cause (e.g. *so*, *because*) • First or third person
Instructions Tell the reader how to do something or make something	• Aim is contained in title • Resources listed in order of use • Method given in sequenced steps • Headings, subheadings, numbers and diagrams are used	• Imperatives are used • You is sometimes used e.g. *When you see ...* • Short sentences containing one instruction • Time connectives • Vocabulary is plain for clarity • Mostly active voice
Information texts Give the reader facts about a particular topic	• Opening is a general statement • Facts are grouped into paragraphs • Headings, diagrams, illustrations and photos are used	• Written in general terms e.g. *cats* rather than *the black cat* • Usually in the present tense • Contain technical vocabulary • Use cause and sequence connectives • Fairly formal style
Explanation texts Tell the reader why or how something happens	• Opening statement to introduce topic • Sequence of steps that explain the topic • Paragraphs, headings and diagrams used • Layout often designed to support understanding	• Can be in the present or past tense • Technical vocabulary likely • Time connectives sometimes used • Use cause and effect connectives and phrases • Impersonal language used
Persuasion texts Try to persuade the reader to think or do something. They present one point of view.	• Opening statement about the issue • Series of arguments to support the issue, usually with statistics and/or evidence	• Mostly in present tense but can vary • Use emotive language • Use connectives related to logic, e.g. *therefore*, *nevertheless*

Text type	Structure	Language features
Discursive texts Present two or more points of view	• Statement of the issue • Arguments for the issue supported by statistics and evidence • Arguments against the issue supported by statistics and evidence • Conclusion containing writer's comments or opinions	• Mainly in the present tense • Mostly uses active voice • Use emotive language • Use connectives related to logic, e.g. *therefore*, *however*
Analysis, including essay writing Presents the reader with a reasoned response to a text or analysis of question or topic	• Title requires debate • There is a statement of the issue • Overview of points followed by discussion of each point • Uses quotations to support points • Conclusion or summary	• Usually uses third person • Present and past tense used • Connectives of contrast and comparison used, e.g. *unless*, *while*, *however* • Connectives of cause and effect used, e.g. *since*, *therefore*, *because* • Technical vocabulary used • Words used to communicate value judgements, e.g. *powerful*, *convincing*

Framework for teaching English

Year 7 objective matching chart to *Access English 1*

	Teaching objectives	Unit in Student Book
WORD LEVEL **Spelling**	1 Vowel choices 2 Pluralisation 3 Word endings 4 Prefixes 5 High-frequency words 6 Apostrophes 7 Key words	22, 23 26 25 24 20 5, 27 28
Spelling strategies	8 Personal spelling 9 Phonemes and syllables 10 Analogy 11 Strategies for learning spellings 12 Using a dictionary 13 Spellcheckers	30 19 19 19 29 –
Vocabulary	14 Word meaning in context 15 Dictionary and thesaurus 16 Unfamiliar words 17 Word classes 18 Qualification and comparison 19 Lexical patterns 20 Connectives 21 Subject vocabulary 22 Words in different languages	3, 4, 6 6 3, 8 4, 16 18 24, 25, 26 9, 12, 13, 17, 18, 20 – –
SENTENCE LEVEL **Sentence construction and punctuation**	1 Subordinate clauses 2 Noun phrases 3 Boundary punctuation 4 Tense management 5 Active or passive voice 6 Resolve ambiguity 7 Speech punctuation	17 16 1, 5, 14, 17 1, 9 9 9 4
Paragraphing and cohesion	8 Starting paragraphs 9 Main point of paragraph 10 Paragraph structure 11 Sentence variety 12 Sequencing paragraphs	1 10, 12 17, 18 17 12
Stylistic conventions of non-fiction	13 a) Information b) Recount c) Explanation d) Instructions e) Persuasion f) Discursive writing 14 Subject conventions	11 9 12 13 16, 17 18 –

	Teaching objectives	Unit in Student Book
Standard English and language variation	15 Vary formality 16 Speech and writing 17 Standard English 18 Sentences in older text	9 9 9 4
TEXT LEVEL – READING **Research and study skills**	1 Locate information 2 Extract information 3 Compare presentations 4 Note making 5 Evaluate sources	3, 8, 10 3, 10 10 10 11
Reading for meaning	6 Active reading 7 Identify main ideas 8 Infer and deduce 9 Distinguish writer's views 10 Media audiences 11 Print, sound and image	2, 3 1, 12, 17 2, 7 3, 18 15 15, 16
Understanding the author's craft	12 Character, setting and mood 13 Non-fiction style 14 Language choices 15 Endings 16 Author attitudes	4, 7 11, 16 6, 7, 8 1 4
Study of literary texts	17 Independent reading 18 Response to a play 19 Poetic form 20 Literary heritage	2, 3 5 8 8
TEXT LEVEL – WRITING **Plan, draft and present**	1 Drafting process 2 Planning formats 3 Exploratory writing 4 Handwriting and presentation	1, 4, 7, 11 1, 2, 3, 10, 11, 12 2, 3, 15 11
Imagine, explore, entertain	5 Story structure 6 Characterisation 7 Narrative devices 8 Visual and sound effects 9 Link writing and reading	1 5 1 6 4
Inform, explain, describe	10 Organise texts appropriately 11 Present information 12 Develop logic 13 Instructions and directions 14 Evocative description	9, 14, 18 11, 12 11, 12 13 7, 16
Persuade, argue, advise	15 Express a view 16 Validate an argument 17 Informal advice	17 17, 18 14
Analyse, review, comment	18 Present findings 19 Reflective writing	18 15

	Teaching objectives	Unit in Student Book
TEXT LEVEL – SPEAKING AND LISTENING Speaking	1 Clarify through talk 2 Recount 3 Shape a presentation 4 Answers, instructions, explanations 5 Put a point of view	2, 3, 10, 12 1 15 12 17
Listening	6 Recall main points 7 Pertinent questions 8 Presentational techniques 9 Oral text types	15 10, 12, 15 16 13
Group discussion and interaction	10 Report main points 11 Range of roles 12 Exploratory talk 13 Collaboration 14 Modify views	8 8 8 8 18
Drama	15 Explore in role 16 Collaborate on scripts 17 Extend spoken repertoire 18 Exploratory drama 19 Evaluate drama presentations	5 5 9 5, 14 5, 15